Cover Illustration by
Phoebe Adams

Smashing through the Glass Ceiling!

True stories of abuse, tragedy and heartache
leading to strength, hope and happiness.

Copyright © 2020 Rebecca Adams

ISBN: 9798555018120
Imprint: Independently published

Published By ICK com. llc Publishing House©

Edited By Rebecca Adams & ICK Publishing
Cover Design and Book Design By ICK Publishing©

Cover Illustration by Phoebe Adams

Smashing Through the Glass Ceiling!
True stories of abuse, tragedy and heartache
leading to strength, hope and happiness.

Smashing Through the Glass Ceiling is a Compilation of
14 International Authors

**This is a work of nonfiction. No names have been changed, no characters
invented, no events fabricated.**

Remember you are
worth more than
rubies & diamonds"

REBECCA ADAMS

IN DEDICATION:

To my beautiful and brave Mum Carole,

You are a tower of strength and so courageous in your journey. I am proud to be your daughter and thank you for showing me the way.
I love you dearly and dedicate this book

"Smashing Through The Glass Ceiling"
to you. xx

Foreword

Vulnerability is Beautiful...

When Rebecca had asked me to write the foreward for this book, I can tell you how humble, honored, and excited I'am. Even though I thought she might think at times am a bit touched. But there's a little crazy in all of us. That's why I don't envy other people's lives. You never know what a person may be masking with their smile. They may look happy, but in reality, they are desperately trying to hide some sorrow or pain. Society expects us to wear this mask – it's what people prefer to deal with or see. But often times taking off that mask is just what we need to do. And it's the bravest thing we can do. Especially if you've dealt with abuse, tragedy and heartache.

Our beautiful broken stories look different, and is different, for those dealing with it and for those who love them. You may have heard many different things about abuse, tragedy, heartache and depression. – based on the misinformation found in movies and the media. For many people, these characterizations couldn't be further from the truth. Don't judge people by what you've seen on social media or what you may have been told.

It's our time we're Smashing through the Glass Ceiling and it's time for you to hear our voices first hand - right here in this book.

In these pages, each author speaks out – telling their journey of dealing with the glass ceiling around their livelihood and their loved ones, and how they learned to smash through the Glass to deal with and grow from their experiences. In each chapter, discover the glassed world of abuse, tragedy and heartache. Most important you will take a journey with these amazing human beings.

My hope and prayers are that in reading this book you open your mind to a new perspective and create a dialogue of understanding. That you learn that the learning and healing journey of abuse, tragedy and heartache, is not linear – but can be a roller coaster.

That life will sometimes look so amazing and other times feel like a black hole, trying to bend you until you break. That you can Smash through the Glass Ceiling and together overcome it, leading to strength, hope and happiness.

If you know someone who needs help, please support them, love them, and contact your local support facility...

Irene Prokopiw

Content

Content

Books Sponsors

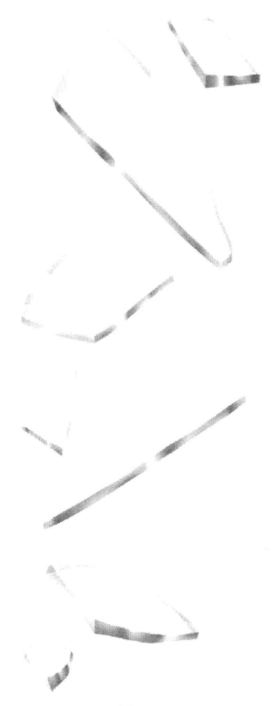

Introduction

This book is for anyone who has been or is going through a struggle in their life and felt like they don't know what to do or how to get through to the other side.

For anyone who has felt like they are a victim to others' decisions and that they have been through so many trials and tribulations that they are constantly being tested.

Maybe you have anxiety, depression, have been through a childhood or relationship with abuse and didn't know how strong you were until being strong was the only choice you had.

Or you have been through something so catastrophic that you had to be your strongest at your weakest moment but didn't give up.

This book is for you.

In life things happen, and you have to know that everything is a test in order to make you bigger, better, bolder, wiser and stronger and also, it's a chance for you to rise up and become your higher self. Some things can't be explained but knowing and trusting yourself – that you are right here, where you're meant to be, and believing that everything works out the way it's supposed to is important, so do know that it's this or something better.

Whatever you are experiencing may feel and appear to be hard and you may feel alone but that's not the feeling or emotion I want you to carry daily. It's not good for you or your mindset or mental health.

Sometimes you may feel that your identity is being taken away and you don't feel like yourself anymore. This could be because of certain people or situations you're in. You may feel hopeless and you may feel as though you're not good enough and not worthy of great things but I'm here to encourage you and to remind you that you are enough, and you are worthy. You have to take the 1st steps of knowing and believing that the universe is guiding and helping you to be the best version of yourself possible.

This book is here to inspire you. Each story is a beautifully written layer of the author's life that they have decided to share with you.

Yes.....you!

Because they may have been where you are – with the overthinking, the sadness, the overwhelm and they have come through the other side of their own trials and tribulations and with this book I want you to know that you can get through your dark days and your heartache and smile again.

You have courage and strength within you to smash through the glass ceiling you may have put above you or that someone else has put there for you. They have showed you their limits and what they think of you but know that you don't have to listen to the haters or negativity that is surrounding you. You have a choice to elevate your beliefs, unlearn all of those BS stories that are holding you back, and maybe have held you back for years, and you can write yourself a new positive and amazingly powerful story of your life.

Remember - Life is precious – you only get one so show up to your life today!

What people say and think defines them not you, and you have to keep the fire in your soul and the stars in your eyes. Go after your dreams and desires and don't hold back for anything – you owe it to yourself.

Release the victim mindset you are in and find the strength within you. I know it's there and it's time for you to level up and live the best life you can possibly live - with pure happiness, joy and filled with kindness and self-respect. You can do it! I believe in you!

One exercise I would love you to do as you read each chapter of this life-changing book, is to write down everything that has been holding you back. All the fears, people, situations, thoughts and everything you can think of. Take your time as it may be emotional for you and that's okay.

Tears are a sign of strength not weakness and they're great for cleansing the soul so if the tears come, let them flow and know it is part of the process.

Then I would like you to read over what you've written. As you read each sentence or paragraph, I would like you to tap into that emotion and thought and feel it. Take your time. With your hand on your heart I would like you to say the H'oponopono Prayer;

"I'm sorry. Forgive me. Thank you. I love you".

And really feel the emotional attachment be released and let it go.

The more that you hold onto negativity the more it becomes overbearing, overwhelming and sad for you. Repeat this a few times for each sentence that you have written and truly know with all your heart, mind, body, soul and mindset that you are finally releasing all of those icky, funky and negative thoughts. It may take a few days or weeks but continuously doing this will help.

The reason why I'm recommending this to you is that it's a clearing technique and also to encourage you to CHOOSE YOU over anything and everything negative.

CHOOSE YOU.
CHOOSE PEACE WITHIN YOURSELF.
PROTECT YOUR ENERGY.
BECAUSE YOU ARE IMPORTANT.
YOU DESERVE TO BE RESPECTED, APPRECIATED AND LOVED.

Take time to reflect on everything positive that's happened in your life. The people you have met, places you have been and all the lives you have touched. Remain present in the moment and come from a place of gratitude always.

"Stay humble and you can get through anything thrown at you."

REBECCA ADAMS

I'd like to share with you something I want you to learn about yourself, is that you are strong and wise. Stay humble and you can get through anything thrown at you.

- Know that you are NOT alone
- Believe you can overcome anything
- Keep your grace and dignity
- Silence IS a response sometimes
- Surround yourself with people who will uplift you
- Work on your mindset (it is paramount)
- Believe in you
- Still wear your heart on your sleeve
- Rise up & be the warrior

Thank you to you, the reader, for investing in yourself and for reading this book of powerful and incredible real stories.

Reflection is everything
Mindset is everything
Happiness is everything
Remember who you are, and the game will change!
You're worth more than rubies and diamonds.

Rebecca Adams. x

99

Life can sometimes be like
a pebble in a shoe.
You have to take the pebble out, get
your walking boots on,
grab that water bottle and live your
most phenomenal life ever because
you only get one, so live it."

REBECCA ADAMS

Shattered Heart

*I collapsed on the kitchen floor in a heap,
crying and wailing.
My heart broke in that moment...*

No....no....no! This can't be happening.

It was October 2011 and I was on my laptop working, when a message popped up to ask if I was related to a 'Ryan Adams'. The message was from America, where Ryan was working and so I replied with a "Yes, we had been married and had a family".

The reply back was shocking. Ryan had gone missing whilst working in Texas and hadn't shown up for work, which if you knew Ryan, you knew America was his massive all-time goal. He'd always wanted to live and work there, so him going missing and not turning up to work was so out of character it was unbelievable to be honest.

The person messaging was his friend who he worked with and so I was brought up to speed with all the details. I then got on the phone to his step-dad in Cornwall who told me he had received a letter about Ryan's work visa being revoked. I phoned his sister and we spoke for hours, and that is when the whole journey began.

I had met Ryan when I was 16yrs old as I joined the British Army and was posted to Aldershot. We clicked straight away, liked the same things (apart from our football teams), had

23

fun, laughed, chatted for hours and started our relationship. As time went on, we split up but got back together, got married and had children. Things went in a different direction and I ended up filing for a divorce, which was one of the testing things I've ever had to do but it needed to be done.

So, when I received this message, I knew there was something wrong immediately as I know Ryan on every level and have done for a long time.

Ryan's cousin set up a Facebook group to find Ryan. We added people who we knew, friends and family and I started adding Army friends and contacts, plus his work colleagues and his old oil rig buddies were added too.

Posters were made, posts were shared over social media and we were also in contact with the Sheriff's department and trying to get information from them as to where they were up to. Day 1 turned into Day 7.

Day 7 turned into Day 14. Still nothing...

I was on my own, with my two children, still working my business every day and now had the task of finding Ryan, together with everyone in the Facebook Group. We had come together as a community to try and find him.

Things weren't as forthcoming as I had hoped, and I took it upon myself to step it all up the "Rebecca Way".

Now, if you know me or have heard anything about me, you will have heard that I am relentless, unstoppable and I keep going until it's done. I don't stop. I don't slow down and I don't waiver.

So, finding Ryan was non-negotiable.

I was sleeping for 4 hours per night, as most of the time I was emailing MP's and Missing Person's companies in London, phoning and emailing America, posting in the Facebook Group daily (counting the days), contacting people and working my business too, as well as school runs, feeding the children and keeping the house going.

Questions were being raised of his timeline as I started to track it. We got a close friend who is a spirit medium to see if she could locate him too. Ryan's mobile phone and bank cards had not been used. He had no ID, no wallet, no passport, no laptop or anything with him. His roommate kept changing his recollection of events. He also said a few things that, as I had known Ryan since I was 16yrs old and had been married to him, I knew they were lies.

> **My emails and phone messages to them went unanswered. I felt like I was banging my head against a brick wall.**

I was updated with his last known whereabouts which was in Austin, Texas on 12th Oct 2011 (before we knew he had gone missing). Again, out of character considering he was supposed to have been at work in Houston. Then, we were informed that his truck had been found in California on Friday 14th Oct 2011, but no-one had heard or seen of him since. Nothing was left in the truck apart from camping gear.

I started to step up the search and contacted the place he was last seen in Texas to see if there was any CCTV or if they could tell me anything. I tracked how long it would take to drive from Texas to California (considering there were no empty food or drink wrappers in the car), how much fuel and what route would be taken, what gas stops etc but no cards were used and no money taken out of the bank account either.

The Sheriff's weren't forthcoming with information and had already taken people into their precinct and questioned them. My emails and phone messages to them went unanswered. I felt like I was banging my head against a brick wall. I felt like I was nagging and moaning but I didn't care. This was a human being who had gone missing and I didn't see any progress being made with the investigation at all.

> **On the inside I was so tired, barely getting sleep (months of living off 4 hours sleep each night), trying to understand what had happened.**

Still, the group, posters, and connections carried on building as I would not let this drop. I HAD to find Ryan – no matter what and no matter how long it took. I had an obligation.

Day 14 turned into Day 30 and then to Day 50. Still nothing....

I always had HOPE. It was a massive thing for me to keep hold of. I never waivered in knowing that he would be found and so the rainbow became my symbol for the journey, for myself, for Ryan and our children.

Ryan's birthday came and went. We thought he would be in contact. But, nothing. We saw Christmas and New Year in all thinking of Ryan. And 2012 started sadly.

Our wedding anniversary was 5th January and so I then decided to put a public post on my personal wall on Facebook (with our wedding photo) to alert everyone I now needed their help (as I had kept everything private to the Facebook group up until this point). But now we needed more eyes on this mission and we needed to step it up.

On the inside I was so tired, barely getting sleep (months of living off 4 hours sleep each night), trying to understand what had happened. I was confused, upset, angry and all of those emotions BUT I vowed to myself not to let the children know anything was wrong. I still did all of my work and the school runs, smiled and jumped on calls that needed to be completed.

On 16th January 2011 I received a private Facebook message from a lady in America...

It was Day 97.

She asked me to contact her regarding information about Ryan and she left a number to phone.

I had just been on the school run so I sorted the children out with snacks, drinks and put the television on and I carried my laptop and phone into the kitchen and closed the door.

I rang the American number she gave me and spoke to a lovely lady who was on a switchboard who couldn't transfer me to the department as the lady who had messaged me hadn't told me what department to contact.

(As I write this now... I'm in floods of tears as I'm catapulted right back into that moment! It's shocking how things creep up on you in a split second. I'm right back in that kitchen as I type this).

I messaged the lady to ask what department to ask for, as I was still on the phone, but she didn't reply straight away so I apologised to the switchboard lady and told her I would ring back as soon as I knew. I hung up the phone.

And......as soon as I did, a message came through... It said...

"CORONER'S DEPARTMENT"!

I collapsed on the kitchen floor in a heap, crying and wailing. My heart broke in that moment...

> I stood in silence. My eyes wide. Everything I had known had disappeared in that split second of talking to a stranger.

'No...no...no! It can't be true. This can't be happening'.

Those thoughts were in my head as tears streamed down my face. Ryan's face in my mind.

At that moment my daughter, who was 8yrs old at the time, tried to come into the kitchen so I had to stop the door from opening, with my feet, wipe my tears and try to change my tone of voice so it sounded like I wasn't crying – something a lot of people can relate to so that others don't know anything is wrong. I gave her a drink and she went back into the living room as I grabbed the phone to ring America once again.

I spoke to the lady on the switchboard who said "Oh I am so sorry honey. My condolences". I was then wired through to the coroner and she told me that they had found a John Doe matching Ryan's description. She had found the Facebook group and chosen to contact me in order to set the process in motion of identifying him and all that goes along with that.

As she was talking to me, my voice was choked. I was in shock and tears were still running down my face. Her words just didn't seem real and even though I was listening to them, as she spoke to me, it felt like I was in a dream – a nightmare in fact.

I wrote everything down she needed me to do and send to her and then said "Thank you" before I put the phone down.

I stood in silence. My eyes wide. Everything I had known had disappeared in that split second of talking to a stranger. Even more questions came into my head and the tears..... oh the tears!

What flashed before me was our entire life together and all our experiences. Until a bolt hit me and I knew I then had to phone his step-dad and sister. Two separate calls I didn't want to do but had to. It was awful – something I wouldn't wish on anyone.

We vowed just to have this day (Day 97) to ourselves as a family to let everyone know and not put anything in the Facebook group. It was ours for the time being to process. His sister told Ryan's dad and everyone was told that night.

Day 98 arrived. I announced in the Facebook group that a body had been found believing to be Ryan. We had to get confirmation, but we would keep everyone updated.

Still my children had no idea anything was going on. A

choice I still stand by today. Unnecessary stress, anxiety and heartache is no good for anyone, let alone children.

The following weeks consisted of me contacting the British Army for dental records, talking to my local police to see how to get DNA from my daughter for America, telling the coroner all details of Ryan – blood type, birthmark, Army regimental number, workplace details, contact details of Texas etc and sending photos to her.

It felt like forever.

I did have one request of the coroner – If she had confirmation, to NOT tell me on 24th January. Leave it until the day after, because that's my birthday and that day would be tarnished forever with bad news.

Telling my children that Ryan had died was the worst thing I've ever done in my entire life.

She kept her promise to me.

And on 29th January 2012 I received confirmation that the body found was Ryan. He was 33yrs old.

The weeks following, consisted of raising money to bring Ryan home for his funeral, trying to get an airline to bring him home, contacting the military charities and the military to help, emailing MP's – all of which said they were sorry, but they could not help. I also had to decide what Californian funeral director's he was going to whilst we did all of this work. We had a deadline that the coroner set but unfortunately Ryan had to be cremated in the end, as the coroner took the decision out of our hands completely. I do understand why.

I nominated his American friend to be in charge of Ryan whilst he was still in America and he had to fill in forms whilst on messenger to me, asking me the questions so that the form could be completed. A very long process to cremate someone and sort it all out as I was thousands of miles away. But it was done.

I decided that in the February half-term that I was going to sit down and tell the children. So, beforehand I had spoken to both schools, prepped the teachers, got counselling in place ready for when they went back to school.

Telling my children that Ryan had died was the worst thing I've ever done in my entire life. As a parent, your job is to protect and guide your children, so I had to be my strongest at my weakest moment and it's not a day I will ever forget. My daughter was 8yrs old and my son was 13yrs old.

Ryan was cremated in America on 19th March 2012. Lots of candles were lit and balloons released, prayers said in all different countries, in all different time zones, by everyone that knew him. I was and am still so grateful for everyone who was on that journey.

Ryan landed on British Soil, in the hands of my British funeral director on 29th March 2012 and remained at the Chapel of Rest until I picked him up on 2nd April 2012.

I had Ryan split into two, and so he was placed in a scattering tube for Cornwall and for Wiltshire I had a wooden box made with his name on the plaque. He was wrapped in a Union Flag and I bought a plot for him in Wiltshire.

My daughter carried Ryan to his grave and I lowered him down with Union Flag ribbon. We had a poem read and it's a sacred place that we do visit.

Ryan was scattered at a beautiful place in Cornwall where we got married (just beyond) and he's free, safe and loved – even now and always will be.

Ryan was full of adventure, life, smiles, jokes and laughter. He lives on and is with us always.

I decided to honour my daughter for her 16th birthday and surprise her at the Empowerment Convention IGNITE Live Event in 2019. I asked an amazing lady singer to sing mine and Ryan's wedding song, so I could dance to it with my daughter.

There wasn't a dry eye in the room, and it was an absolutely beautiful moment that we will both cherish forever. https://youtu.be/BM_uFFZ7uCs

My message to you, from me finally writing this chapter of my life, is that LIFE IS PRECIOUS and so you have to be full of gratitude every single day.

Your life is important, as when you pass away, it's the dash on your headstone that symbolises your life. So, really think about what you're going to achieve and how many lives you can positively change whilst you're here.

People and experiences are going to test you but know that you CAN get through anything and YOU ARE STRONG.

You can choose to elevate, rise up and don't let anything negative define you. Do what aligns with you and with what feels great. Fill your purpose and destiny with focusing on your happiness.

Build the empire, travel, dance like no-one is watching and lead with kindness always.

Do not stop. Do not waiver and Believe in you. You have one life so go live it!

And finally, from me to you - my all-time mantra that I live and breathe...

KEEP GOING ALWAYS™

**I dedicate this chapter to my two amazing children
and
my incredible Mum
I love you dearly.**

**I also dedicate this chapter to everyone who
was part of this 6-month journey
I appreciate you all.**

**Finally, I dedicate this chapter to Ryan
I never stopped looking for you. x**

Rebecca Adams

Rebecca Adams

Rebecca Adams wears her heart on her sleeve and always flows in alignment through her life and business. She kicks ass at what she does, and she is focused on empowering as many people as possible to feel alive and live a phenomenal life through gaining control of their mindset.

Her mission is to give more people the mindset, skillset and tools to gain more clarity, focus and confidence to master their life in all areas.
Rebecca has been in business for over 17 years and she is all about empowering, inspiring and motivating people to uplevel, rise up, be a voice and to trust the process. She lives and breathes the Law of Attraction daily and is focused on giving as much value as possible to her audience.

She is the International Life & Business Mastery Mentor™ for people who want to create personal and financial freedom. She is an International Mindset Coach & Mentor, Law of Attraction Practitioner, NLP Practitioner, Belief Clearing Practitioner, Author, Speaker, Motivator and Business Woman. She also builds websites.

Rebecca changes people's lives through her Transformational Digital Online Programs, High-end Private Bespoke Coaching & Mentoring. She also has an online membership club named Ignite Academy which is jampacked full of amazing content.
She is also the Creative Director & Founder of the Empowerment Convention IGNITE Live Event which is a life-changing event with speakers, a gala dinner and entertainment, held annually in the Roman City of Bath, UK.

Rebecca is an award-winning entrepreneur, #1 International best-selling co-author, and masters in mindset. Unlike every other personal development expert, she focuses on aligning every area of your life so that you can take control and have everything you desire.

She is a Mum to 2 amazing incredible human beings, a Special Needs Mum, a UK Army Veteran and she lives in the UK. She loves to travel, read, listen to music, take photographs, watch movies and make endless memories.

WEB LINKS:
Website: https://www.rebeccaadamsbiz.com
Business Facebook Page: https://www.facebook.com/rebeccaadams187
Personal Facebook Wall: https://www.facebook.com/rebecca.adams.39108/
Online Digital Course Website: http://racourses.thinkific.com/
Linktree: https://linktr.ee/rebeccaadams187
Instagram: https://www.instagram.com/rebeccaadams187
Pinterest: https://www.pinterest.com/rebeccaadams187

,,

Hold faith in the yet unseen,
take inspired action and maybe
not tomorrow but one day
what was once invisible
becomes visible"

ALISON PARSONS

How did I get here?

No.... not how did I get here fulfilling my dreams as a Multi Passionate Entrepreneur.

Well yes, how did I get here but how did I get from thinking the world was my oyster... to dropping the kids off at school and then huddling in the corner of the sofa and wishing the world would go away?

In 1995, things weren't going to plan. As a teenager - the shy "Yes Girl, don't rock the boat, do as you're told 'pleaser disease' girl" was finally embarking on her dream of Higher Education. During that time, I found myself in a lecture where an artist told us everything is energy, nothing is solid (including the chairs we were sat on). It was all just balls of energy vibrating at different frequencies.

My fellow students ridiculed him. I stood silently not knowing why. But felt in my gut what he said was true. Once again, I felt like the outsider because I was seeing things differently, like my first day of college when I was sent on an assignment. Everyone came back with degradation and negativity - I saw beauty and positivity.

Little did I know how relevant all this would be.

Fast forward to my Course Finals where I had to submit my subject matter by a certain date, and I had absolutely zilch. Well, almost nothing.

With the new millennium fast approaching, there were a lot of New Age philosophies being bandied about and I was fascinated why so-called "New Age subject's" were in fact thousands of years old. I was feeling overwhelming fear of the deadline and nothing to submit and went to a calm trust that everything would be alright.

I was becoming aware of occasions in my life where sequences of events would occur, everything would work out in my favour and I had a knowing inside the same thing was going to happen. And it did, but more incredible than I could ever have imagined, and this is all documented in my book "Blue Bridge, Yellow Van".

Fast forward to the Private View which my Lecturers assigned me to curate, despite the belligerent bunch of mature students I shared my course with. I stood talking to some very influential guests who asked to meet me because they liked my work. Everything seemed perfect. I felt like I was floating, like the day my Finals idea came to me, and when I was working on them.

Have you ever had that sensation?

Then enters, I shall call him Dave, for the purpose of this book, who out of all my fellow students was the most temperamental and became very loud and unpleasant when he didn't get his own way.

He glared at me and bulldozed the conversation, forcefully trying to direct the guests talking to me over to his work.

The atmosphere became uncomfortable and eventually he persuaded the guests to look at his work with his relentless interruptions. I was brought back down to earth and everything felt dark and heavy. The worst thing was, I allowed it.

After University I remembered the positive parts of that conversation and felt inspired that I would land a great opportunity and my career would finally start but after several knockbacks I stopped trying.

I was a single mum of three children on assistance and with a roof over our head. I used to drop the children to school, close the blinds, ignore the telephone and pretend I wasn't home. Scared of everything and nobody knew.....until now.

I became clever.

I opened the blinds before picking the kids up. Had every excuse under the sun of why I hadn't answered the phone "sorry you called? I must have been hanging out the washing" And put on a bright smiley face.

> I blamed the system for keeping me trapped on welfare and I would try when they were older.

I stopped looking for a job saying the kids are too young and if I got a job, I would be worse off. I blamed the system for keeping me trapped on welfare and I would try when they were older.

A while later, my drive came back and with it another sequence of events in my favour and beyond my belief. Followed by another crash and here I was again with the blinds shut and the telephone unplugged with my hood over my head.

These days I would be labelled with anxiety and depression, but I hadn't heard of those titles then and I wasn't aware of what I was in, in the midst of it - a subconscious reaction to a set of circumstances.

The irony was I had become an avid reader of Personal Development books after being handed a copy of "Feel the Fear and Do it Anyway" by Susan Jeffers. It did change my life, but I soon referred back to old thought patterns and tried another book.

With each book I always believed my life would change but again, normality would kick in and I would reach for the next book.

Finally, in 2010 I had A lightbulb moment!!

Somehow, in this timeframe I had managed to become an Operations Manager and still desperately unhappy. Until that eventful day where my whole world crashed from the sudden death of a close friend and being bullied by a colleague. I found myself speaking to a God I didn't believe in saying, "If you don't stop this pain, I'm outta here".

As soon as I said that, I kid you not, I felt a voice say; "Find the article you have hidden away". Not being in a position to read said article I put it away then forgot about it.

99

I felt a voice say;
"Find the article
you have
hidden away."

As I wandered around, something turned my focus onto a pile of magazines and there tucked inside was the article. I read how a soap actress had made her dreams come true and attributed to something she learnt from the book "The Secret".

I logged onto Amazon, and from that moment on, my mood lifted, and I felt hopeful again despite not actually having the book.

On its arrival, I read all about positive and negative thoughts and how we attract our experiences from these thoughts. Everything is energy, just as I heard over a decade previously that resonated to me and not my peers. That is when I then truly appreciated, for the first time, the term - Law of Attraction.

I realized where I was going wrong.

I jumped into each book looking for answers but never actually actioned any of the teachings. Slowly but surely, I started to do certain things in the book. One of my favourites was and still is, Affirmations.

-Did my change take place overnight? (like some may read in this book), "No it didn't".

-

Was I perfect? "No, I kept falling back into old negative thought patterns and the classic "This stuff doesn't work". (which is an affirmation in itself).

But now armed with the terminology The Law of Attraction and my passion for reading I kept reading more books on the subject.

"I'm still learning" Michelangelo aged 87

I kept implementing their teachings and I started to see the pattern of the Law of Attraction throughout my whole life and this created faith in the yet unseen. So, I started a blog called The Law of Attraction Lover" in 2013 to hopefully inspire others.

One of my favourite contributors to the book and film "The Secret", was Bob Proctor and I used to listen to his YouTube videos over and over again on my commute. Bob talked of how he was advised to make a Goal Card with a goal he wanted to achieve and read it as often as he could. This inspired me to do the same. I had always dreamed of being self-employed so that's what I put on my card.

"I am successfully self-employed doing what I love and loving what I do"

Did things instantly get better? No, they got significantly worse.

The next day I broke my leg in 3 places requiring an operation, making me miss my daughter's wedding in Jamaica, but somewhere deep inside I found strength and faith. There was a bigger picture to all of this, and my thinking must have been seriously off to attract this and more importantly nobody died so I could live with it.

"Sangfroid" dictionary meaning = composure or coolness shown in danger or under trying circumstances

A short time after this event I was due to be 50 and had lots of exciting plans to celebrate, including going to New York for New Year's Eve and climbing the Statue of Liberty. I was not excited about the prognosis of 12 to 18 months for my leg to get as good as it was going to get though.

During these years since finding The Secret, I had also found Dr. Wayne Dyer and he introduced me to Anita Moorjani's book "Dying to be Me" and that still small voice that I had become accustomed to whispered in my mind as I re-read this book.

Anita talks of her self-healing and I secretly decided to fully heal myself so I could enjoy my trips.

I write about this story often on social media to hopefully inspire others that you can start living your life of Freedom and Joy at any age, in any circumstance and as I write this today it's the 4th Anniversary of me breaking my leg. We are currently going through an unprecedented time in history as the world is in lockdown (due to Covid-19) and the Earth seems to be 20 years later being forced to live the theme of my Art Finals theme, which was actually about taking time in our busy lives to stop and appreciate the little things in life and live in Gratitude.

I digress. Or do I? As I see a huge pattern and that, irrelevant of Newtonian-based time, every single little thing as Anita explains in her book is linked like a huge tapestry.

So, going back to my secret leg-healing episode. Not a word was shared of my healing project as I didn't want to allow anyone to talk me out of it or affect my energy by telling me it was not possible. Learning from those episodes 20 years earlier at the private viewing, everything is either a lesson or a blessing.

Our number one priority is ***"Protect Your Energy"***.

After the initial operation, nothing was planned for several weeks so I set about meditating on my healing and working on a book (the oddly named one above I mentioned) I had started previously. However, the Universe had different plans and I started divine downloading another book about The Law of Attraction and Bullying. Something I had experienced as a child, teenage and adult. Remember.....Blessing or a Lesson.

Sat awaiting an X-ray, my partner asked a member of staff what happens now. The reply was, "The consultant will look at the X-rays. The leg may need to go back in a cast or a boot". When my name was called, before I even had fully entered the room the consultant said, "Well I am pleased to tell you that you have healed incredibly well"

I was silent taking it in. I had done it!

"Start walking on it slowly and refer back to crutches if you feel you need them. You will need some physio" the consultant said. That was it, apart from saying I would need another appointment in a few weeks, just to check everything was still okay and to sign me off.

The physio appointment? Signed off at the first meeting by bemused physio mumbling something about never seeing someone in my position have such flexibility in their ankle after an accident like this and there's nothing I really need to do for you.

The downside was that I had to return to work faster than I had anticipated, halting the book. I could not have foreseen the chaos that confronted me, that had developed in my absence with my team but each and every morning I placed my neglected 'Goal Card' in front of my PC. I wrote affirmations, listened to motivational material as I drove to work and read as often as I could but that was about it

Bob also says, "when you have a goal - the way and the how are not our business. The Universe takes care of that". Remember what I said previously about seeing a pattern in my life of things working out better than I ever anticipated.

After a few weeks, I handed my notice in and then a short time later, after my trip to the top of the Statue of Liberty, a friend started a Facebook page around a new hobby she had started called LoveDucks. She got so inundated by requests for her creations she couldn't keep up due to other business responsibilities and initially put out that she was stopping and then changed her post to offering it as a Business Opportunity.

I jumped into Driving Instructor Training as a source of being self-employed, but Bob Proctor taught me successful people have multiple streams of income. So, I jumped on that opportunity. I feel somehow that friend was inspired to start this hobby as part of the Universe's plan to give me the business I so longed for.

I soon noticed I started to feel sick during driving lessons and time moved like molasses. However, if I was working on any LoveDucks time it flew like Einstein time.

This was the feeling I had when I was painting my canvasses for my Art degree Finals. I wished I could do this full time and not do the driving. Having this enlightenment, I decided like my Art Finals to surrender this to the Universe and then as the saying goes Ask, Believe, Receive and I wasn't wrong.

Yet again a sequence of events happened so awesomely beyond prediction. I was presented with a Network Marketing opportunity and LoveDucks shop idea all in less than 24 hours.

Despite having multiple examples of the Law of Attraction in action this sealed the deal that this stuff is real, and I just wanted to share the message more than ever. You can live your life of Freedom and Joy.

After setting an intention to create an income that allowed me more location-freedom and to travel in a matter of days, the Universe supplied again. A service-based opportunity that is in travel.

I can honestly say I have met the most incredible people in my life today, outside of my oldest friends and family. They all came about from connections made via the Network Marketing space including the incredible Rebecca Adams.

What I didn't expect when I joined the industry is the community. These people openly spoke of their love of Personal Development, listened to YouTube videos, wrote affirmations, believed in the Law of Attraction and shared it freely and they gave me the courage to become my truest, most authentic self, regardless of what anyone else thought, which funnily enough was an affirmation I had.

Jumping from the hooded huddle to the present day at the time of writing this, I still have the LoveDucks shop and online business, I am involved in Network Marketing. I am an Advanced Law of Attraction Practitioner, Master Life Coach and Art therapist, author, speaker, blogger with many other projects in the pipeline and an enthusiastic Lover of Life and on a mission now to help Woman create Financial Independence to live lives of guess what?! ......Freedom and Joy!!!

This is my dedication -
"To anyone who thinks you can't, You Can"

Alison Parsons

Alison Parsons

Alison Parsons is a multi-faceted person who is currently an Advanced Law Of Attraction Practitioner, Artist, Duck Painter, Author, Network Marketer and Shop Owner. She has just qualified as a Life Coach. She is also in the travel industry.

She helps people to use the Law of Attraction to create lives of freedom and joy.

WEB LINKS:

Personal Facebook page: https://www.facebook.com/alison.k.parsons

Business Facebook Page: www.facebook.com/alisonkparsonsloalover

Instagram: www.instagram.com/alison_k_parsons

LinkedIn: www.linkedin.com/alison-k-parsons-47302716a

Website: http://www.alisonkparsons.com

"

Let the voice within you call for help.
Let the voice within you
give you strength.
Let courage guide you home."

RAY COATES

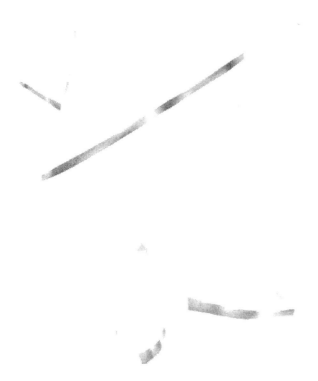

Releasing the Voice Within

'Feel you're stumbling in the shadows;
life has drawn the light from your bones.
Then let this be for you,
let courage guide you home.
Your voice it feels like an echo, life's hand has
dealt you this pain.
Then let this be for you, let hope guide you
through dark rain.
Let the voice within you call for help.
Let the voice within you give you strength.'

How can you sum up an entire life in just a few words? What would you say? What words would you use? Well, the above goes some way to defining one of the most pivotal, life-changing periods of my life.

The voice is such an integral part of us and in 2008, I lost mine for an entire year!

What happened was the single most defining, catalyst that developed my appreciation for the voice (mine and others). In 2008 I was diagnosed with throat cancer!

How did my throat cancer manifest? I was shaving one day and noticed a lump on the side of my neck. I didn't think too much of it initially. I was married at the time, with five children and working full-time as a driving instructor. Life was busy, to say the least. However, over the period of a couple of weeks, the lump got larger.

I decided, after a couple of colds, several very sore throats and the fact my voice kept disappearing, to go to my local GP. Thankfully, for me, my GP had a background in ENT oncology. I remember vividly to this day, after she had examined my neck, my GP asked me, 'what do you think it is'?

> **I remember vividly to this day, after she had examined my neck, my GP asked me, 'what do you think it is'?**

This question baffled me.

You are the doctor I thought. Yet, I knew. I had a deep feeling within me that something in my body was happening. Something was not right. It felt at times like my body was a ticking clock.

I replied to her question, as I took a deep breath and composed my inner feelings, 'well I guess you tend to think the worst.' To which she replied, 'we cannot rule out cancer'!

That moment told me what I already knew. When she confirmed my minds concern, everything stopped. I can't even remember what she said after that.

The truthful realisation of the possibility of cancer, echoed in my head again and again. 'We cannot rule out cancer'! 'We cannot rule out cancer'! 'We cannot rule out cancer'! As I walked back home her words kept repeating.

At that time, we lived very near to the surgery. The total realisation hit me, and it was the beginning of me descending into myself. I guess this was my body's way of preparing me for that which was to come. I was bunkering into myself, battening down the hatches, preparing for battle. She knew and I knew. I have no doubt of that! Looking back now, I always knew ahead of schedule.

After a throat endoscopy (where I had a microfibre camera pushed up my left nostril and down my throat, with no anaesthetic) and a full panendoscopy (under general anaesthetic), I waited for the prognosis.

A week or so later, myself and my then wife, attended a consultation. We joked and laughed about the possibility that it would be funny if I just had tonsillitis. I remember the jokes were for her sake, not mine. Internally, I was already prepared for this consultation.

We entered the room and there was my consultant and also a Macmillan nurse, I thought this is a bit unusual. We were then told, in a very calm and conservative manner, that a 'malignant tumour had formed within my tonsils and it had spread to the lymph nodes in my neck'! Immediately, my wife broke down into tears. She sobbed her heart out.

Whilst I had felt, in the deepest fibre of my body, that I already knew, this was now the sledgehammer of reality. It hit hard!

I had to console my wife, whilst at the same time feeling - I couldn't even trust my own body anymore. Being told of my cancer made me feel my body had been invaded! I was told without preventative treatment, which included major surgery (at least a four-hour procedure) and radiotherapy (for 6 weeks, every day), I would only have a couple of months to live! I remember the Macmillan nurse telling my then wife, 'this will be a belt and braces treatment for him.' I wondered why she was telling her and not me. Later I would discover why.

I was scared, even though I was somehow prepared. It felt like I was falling deep into a dark reality, but I had to try to remain a light for those around me. Especially my children. In truth, I was lost.

I remember returning home and sitting the children down. Our daughters would have then been aged 15, 12, 9 and my sons would have been 3 and 4 years old, respectively. This was another moment where my despair had to be shelved.

I recollect their little faces looking up at me. I was a strong fit man and here I was in a bubble of controlled, level-headed communication to explain calmly to my children that their Dad has got cancer. They responded in the way I set for them - controlled and level-headed. However, inside I was screaming in fear! The beginning of 'The Voice Within'.

As I explained to family and friends of my diagnosis, this began to make me somewhat detached from my own feelings and in hindsight this helped me to dig deeper into my inner resolve.

When you are experiencing something like this, it is very difficult for others to understand and this created a depth in me that I know still exists. It's like an inner home, an inner palace. As I continued to strive to deal with my body and the extreme radiation treatment I received. Moments began to matter more. Breathing mattered. I had the full realisation - I am mortal!

The next period of time was difficult to say the least. I felt like a spectator in my own life.

The doctors pre-warned me of the symptoms of the radiation treatment. Including extreme blistering and resultant infection, from the radiation; virtually total loss of saliva, loss of taste and loss of voice for at least several months. In fact, I had to sign a disclaimer that I accepted I may lose my life (the surgery involved cutting very close to the right subclavian artery). At best I could lose my sense of taste permanently and very potentially my voice forever!

How could I sign something like this?
What would my future be?
Would it be better for everyone else and me if I declined?

At times my mind felt like thousands of people were all shouting different things to me at the same time. My spirit began to feel like it was breaking. I was fragile but needed to go through this potential torture for everyone else.

As I signed, I may as well have written: 'I LOVE MY WIFE & CHILDREN', because this treatment was not for ME but rather, for THEM!

My radiation treatment involved a mask (this was a special plastic that was moulded to my face - it felt like suffocation when it was moulded) and being bolted down by the neck to a radiation table. It felt like medieval torture. The nurses were amazing though. They even said in advance I could bring in my own favourite CDs to listen to during the procedure.

As the weeks went by (a treatment of 30 minutes, 5 days a week for 6 weeks), the music faded into the background. I focused on my children's faces and as I was bolted down, unable to move, I went through the darkest of tunnels mentally, emotionally and physically, for them!

> **I was fragile but needed to go through this potential torture**

I remember a couple of weeks into radiation being out with my children and we were all enjoying burgers at a restaurant. As I began to progressively eat the burger, with each mouthful of it, the taste diminished to the point where it was like eating cardboard and I struggled to chew as well. You may as well have served me the box the burger came in and no I was not 'loving it'! Eating became an ordeal. It was a question of daily just trying to take calories in. Food is far more than just fuel. A meal can be such a social time and taste is an amazing gift.

During this time, my experience made me feel more and more isolated. I spent time temporarily living with my aging Mother and also my then in-laws, as my wife couldn't cope with the extreme pain I went through as a result of the 'belt and braces' treatment.

Did I feel alone? Completely!

I would often be awake all night as my mouth bled and I struggled to breathe, I had a portable nebuliser but it didn't seem to help me breathe any easier. Eating continued to be an ordeal.

My experience made me feel more and more isolated.

Over these months of treatment, I lost more weight. As a result of this, the medical team recommended that I had surgically implanted a feeding plug. This procedure required that I be heavily sedated, then the doctor would insert down my throat and pull out through my stomach a feeding tube! I am a strong man, stronger than at times I realise, a strength I would later rely on, as I became even more disconnected. Well to complete this part of my experience, I fought the medical staff off, as they endeavoured to fit the plug! I was not even aware of this. I rejected this procedure, even though I was heavily sedated. Subsequently, they stopped the procedure, and I had to continue to absorb as many calories as I could force down my narrowing throat.

Those around me said 'you're lucky to be able to pour cream on everything'.

I was in silence! Silence was my life! There was nothing 'lucky' about this experience.

Isn't it wonderful to tell someone: 'I love you'; 'I like you'; 'thank you'.

Nothing! No words!

Yes, I could write things down but as a result of a loss of understanding (also other factors) of those I held close, including my then wife, as a living soul, I began to vanish.

I lost easily a year of my life physically to the cancer treatment. I also experienced deep depression and as a result of other factors, my marriage broke down leading to separation and ultimately divorce.

Additionally, prior to my marriage break up, I received a hand delivered letter (through the letterbox) from my Dads 2nd wife, telling me that my Dad died, who I had not seen from the age of five and at this time I was 43 years of age. Apparently, my Dad and his 2nd wife lived 45 minutes away from where I was living. I never saw him for 38 years! I never saw him again.

Needless to say, 2008 was a VERY difficult period of my life. The solitude and silence of my journey was all consuming. It felt in that year, I lost everything!

Days blurred into one and even after improving in my physical voice and the wounds of surgery and radiation began to heal, the emotional scars of abandonment of my wife and then my Dad, did not.

I descended into what I can now describe as a self-imposed exile for a few years. It was a deeply dark period of my life, as I came to terms with a number of extreme crossroads, all converging at the same time. There were many other limiting situations to deal with too, and it seemed impossible to even string 2 or 3 words and emotional sentences together.

However, over time; what felt like an endless period of time, led me to the realisation - I needed to forgive me and others and allow myself to release my inner voice.

It took time to ascend my inner voice from the descended depths contained within me. Release had to happen. Release often felt judged though. This judgement came from a constant inner voice that masqueraded in my mind as an outer voice, until I learnt it was actually my mind that needed to change.

In the last couple of years, I have moved my mind and as a result my voice, vision and purpose have achieved much more clarity.

Whilst it is important to consider others, we are here and stand as an individual voice on this planet Earth.

I have been able to achieve things in the last couple of years I would not have possibly imagined previously. Through elevating my mindset and by enabling myself to be me, I am allowing myself to be the truly inspired passionate and creative individual that I am. This is by removing from my life anything that will block and cause a hindrance to my greater purpose!

The truly beautiful experience of this is that I am now using my voice to harmonise with others and to help others. So rather than feeling a lone voice, a lost voice, I can now truly see my ability to influence and inspire.

At times there will be judgement, sometimes even those close to us may be negative. Time passes, the journey continues, YOUR voice, however you communicate it, is precious.

I am grateful that cancer taught me to value my life and voice even MORE. I am thankful all of my experiences, even the perceived negative ones, because they have made me even MORE me.

I can see this from my children and from those around me who want to be influenced by my voice. I am eternally grateful to Rebecca Adams for noticing me and deeply encouraging me to step into my purpose.

Is the Journey over?
Not even close to the ultimate destination!
Am I enjoying the Journey? Ohhhh YES!

Additionally, and importantly, I now value the challenges and obstacles I have faced even more.

Was I REALLY a lost voice? No!

We are ALWAYS where we are. Being lost is a perception.

Many, sad to say, in society feel voiceless. We, on a personal, individual basis can and have at times, likely felt voiceless.

Dear reader, if that's how you feel NOW, then let my story encourage you. No matter how trapped you may feel in any circumstances, in any situation, whatever it is, you can find not only escape but more importantly release. You can not only survive but more importantly overcome, conquer and be VICTORIOUS!

I have a vision. I have a mission and so do YOU!

I have full intention to use my inner voice, to use it continually for the remainder of my life for greater good.

Take your next step and may divine love continue to amplify your voice and enable you to fully release that voice in your life journey.

Contributed with heartfelt gratitude to the work, example and personal mentoring of Rebecca Adams.

Ray Coates

Ray Coates

Ray Coates is a singer and songwriter, poet, public speaker and an actor. He is also a throat cancer survivor of over 10 years! He is passionate about creativity and using this as a means to amplify the voice of others. He has been a singer songwriter for 40 years and has released an originally written charity single 'The Voice Within' in 2010 to raise funds and awareness of head and neck cancer.

Additionally, Ray has used this song for 'The Voice Within Project'. This is a project to connect people from diverse backgrounds by means of ONE song and ONE voice. 'The Voice Within' has been performed by singer Zoe Evans and was used to raise funds and awareness for the homeless prevention organisation Shelter.

Ray has reached out to a global audience which led him to come into contact with Charles Mattocks, award winning film maker, and best selling author. Charles asked Ray to write, sing and record a song for his cancer docuseries programme 'Eight Days' which was aired on major networks in USA in April 2020. The song that Ray wrote & recorded 'Your Journey' is available for download on all digital download platforms: Ray released his album 'Garden of Life' in May 2020 for download and on CD.

He designed, built and released an online Songwriting/writing program 'Writing YOUR Unique DNA Songs' earlier this year and also released an ebook of inspirational poetry 'Your GLAD Journey Companion' with his partner in rhyme Michelle Roche at the end of August 2020. Ray is a weekly YouTube vlogger and also carries out a weekly blog through his website.

As well as 2 weekly episodes on his IGTV series 'Be YOU With Me - Connecting in ONE Voice'. Ray continues to write & record personalised signature songs for individual clients and he has future plans to write a children's book. Additionally, he is a guest speaker at the Empowerment Convention Ignite Live event on April 16 & 17 2021 in the City of Bath.

WEB LINKS.

Personal Facebook page: https://www.facebook.com/ray.coates.129

Business Facebook page: https://www.facebook.com/voiceforcancer/

Instagram: https://www.instagram.com/raycoatesvoice

Twitter: https://www.twitter.com/raycoatesvoice

Website: https://www.raycoatesvoice.com/

"

I am beyond my diagnosis
and imperfectly me"

ANGIE CANDLER

Why did I start this?

Well, I can tell you that I never thought in a million years I would have.

You see, I had a great career. I had no problems in the sense of being stuck at home, not having to worry about how I'm going to pay my next bill at the end of the month, but then, something drastic happened.

My life changed forever.

I could no longer be that person who could commute to work, as slowly over the months, I lost that ability, and was eventually told that I no longer had a job due to my illness. So, I was medically retired, which is understandably the way it should have been because I couldn't fulfil my job 100%.

What a shock! What was I going to do? I had worked all my life. My routine was messed up and I wasn't bringing any money into the house.

Days turned into weeks and then into months. My health was going downhill and I was in excruciating pain daily.

I found myself, two years down the line, pretty much housebound, with the only occasion of maybe going out to a family event, hospital or doctor's appointment, which the medical appointments were the majority of the time. I found that going from being an active person out in the world and doing things without worrying about the pain, to being housebound, and whose health is deteriorating by the day, would be testing to say the least but I knew I had to survive.

How was I going to do this? There had to be a way that I could contribute to people's lives without having to leave the house. There had to be a way that I could earn money. I thought to myself, "You know, you're not a silly girl. You've got all these amazing ideas in your head. Let's get this sorted". So that is where my new life and business began.

When you're faced with life-changing circumstances there does come a point where you do question yourself, especially as the negative emotions and thoughts do creep in your head. You find yourself getting dropped by friends, family and also doctors sometimes, who eventually don't want to listen to what's going on in your life or they don't invite you to anything because they know it's quite difficult for you. It can become quite isolating!

This does make you feel insignificant and worthless, but I knew that I could make something of my ideas and so, I trusted in myself and went for it. I started studying and practising mindfulness. I knew I needed to have a stronger mindset than what I had.

Some days were tougher than others as my foggy brain took hold somedays! You know, that feeling of forgetting what you have just said and on those days I rested and listened to my body. When your body is screaming at you and you feel worse because you're trying to be a super being – I knew I had to stop that otherwise I wouldn't be able to get through this. I passed with distinctions and became a mindfulness master practitioner and then started my own vegan refill skincare company. Both of these niches are totally in line with myself because of all of my allergies and severe weirdness that most people generally don't have.

I knew mindset was the key to surviving these health issues. So, if it's going to help me, it's going to help a lot of other people right! The ideas started to flow, and I started to get excited about life again, and I knew that if I got my products out to more people, I could help them and make their life easier and help them to feel great.

> **I have an attitude full of gratitude.**

Once I have an idea in my head, as I'm so strong-willed, I don't stop, and I persevere no matter what. All the skills I've learned over my years in my career have helped me to get to this point and so I knew that I could do this. I went for it and I've not stopped since.

I refuse to let anything hold me back! I have an attitude full of gratitude.

Another obstacle showed itself to me - I was finding it really hard to get out there and network with people. So, I asked myself "what do you do when you're stuck in a situation where you can't get out of the house?" The answer that came to me was that you might buy a ticket to go to a networking event, but then a question came to me again of, "what happens if you wake up that morning and you're not able to get out of the house?"

Well, that was happening to me more often and I was finding myself getting more down about it, because I was thinking about how to connect with others, especially outside of my circle? How am I going to help others if I'm struggling? I'm sure as hell there's a lot more people like myself that are struggling. So, I decided I needed to do something about it!

We all have choices – give up and allow the darkness to keep holding you back OR say Hell no! Not today!

My body might be knackered but my biggest tool was alive and raring to go!

There was nothing out there for people that had disabilities, whether they were on show or hidden. People who have anxiety, depression, people who might not be able to walk properly. They might be in a wheelchair or may have a severe illness that makes them fatigued. I have majority of most of those issues so I can relate to a lot of people. I thought that this is it! I have to create an online platform.

99

I have majority of most of those issues so I can relate to a lot of people.

I got together with my lovely friend Jenny who has MS and discussed with her my idea. We spoke about not just targeting the UK, but the entire world because the idea has no boundaries! If we take this platform online and bring in people that want to help with training, that can give advice on certain aspects to make people feel better, be mindfully aware that this is not the end of their life, that they can do something for themselves, if they had the right mindset then we can help people internationally.

So here I was within a few years of being medically retired, having no job to go to, my career that I knew of ended and me now being housebound, to actually thinking on a grander scale of how I, together with other people like myself, can impact and help so many other people. I started to create a website. Amazing, right? Who would have thought it!

We started off thinking that we were going to channel the people that we know and see how we can get this out there. It would be a platform to help like-minded people who are struggling, because they have these ailments, these disabilities, but we're not letting them define us, because if we do, we might as well just give up. So, what is the point?

As you may have realised, I don't do "giving up", and we have to think outside the box, don't we? We need to. We have to think - what can we do for ourselves today? How can I make my life better for myself, my family, and for other people that might be needing my services?

So here I was sat thinking about how I could change my disappointments and the circumstances I couldn't control around into my favour that I will not be beaten. I will not give up and I won't allow my disability to stop me from doing what I want to do and also making a change in someone else's life.

Sometimes, you have to have a moment to yourself, in the quietness of the day to evaluate everything you have done, where you want to go and what you want to achieve without all the noise.

You have to know and believe that anything can change in an instant, like it did with me. But did it stop me? No! My life just took a different direction and that's okay. This is about my life.

This is about your life.

Maybe you have been given awful news and you don't know how to deal with it, may not know what you're going to do, and you may be thinking you don't have anyone to talk to. I am here to tell you that you are not alone. I want you to know, with my story, that you can make something happen with your life no matter what. You just have to choose.

Don't feel like it is the end because you have had bad news. Take time for yourself, to think and to regain your strength. Yes, it's life-changing and sometimes you can't turn it around. So, the question is then given to you – what are you going to do?

You can be yourself, with your ponytail, your beard, your tattoos. You can make a change no matter what your diagnosis is. It doesn't mean because you have a label, like me, that you stop living. It means that you need to work on yourself to embrace the new you, if that makes sense.
Bad days are going to happen, as are good days too. But, it's in the bad days that you find the light that gets you through – maybe it's a person, maybe it's a place or maybe it's a song. Some days are harder than others, some days we just need someone to say; "I get it! I understand and you are not alone. I'm here for you. I will listen to you".

When something like this happens to you and it's out of your control, you do have to mourn the life that would have been for you. Because your life is now taking a different path and you have new obstacles to overcome and new-found strength to find too.

As long as the right people are around you, it makes a huge difference to your life and how you live it. You want to be respected and appreciated, regardless of the disability that you have.

You are still alive, and you matter!

It's wonderful when people come together and be that friendly ear in times of woe, to form friendships, offer advice and people who you can learn from. The joy of the internet opens everyone up to a world of possibilities, especially if you're housebound, like me. It truly is a gift that I use daily to give back and help others from around the world, so that's a positive thing that I focus on too.

I want you to know that it is okay having a disability and it is okay to cry sometimes but knowing that you can come from a place of love and use the skills you know (like myself from my previous career) to create something new and exciting. That is what you're here to do and it's wonderful when the disability community can come together and make change (whether it's a hidden disability or not).

I'm not saying it's easy and I do have awful days where I have to stop, sleep and slow down and I will say, I have never been the same person since my diagnosis and I have a lot of health issues now, but I know I can help so many people globally with what I'm creating and it makes me smile every day – no matter how much pain I'm in.

Don't let your disability hold you back from doing anything. It may slow you down but still try and find a goal or dream that you want to fulfil and find people to help you along the way, if you need to.

> **"**
> We are strong and resilient and won't stop helping others through generosity, sheer kindness of the soul of wanting to help people.

We are a global family of creators, changing lives because our life changed in a split moment. We are strong and resilient and won't stop helping others through generosity, sheer kindness of the soul of wanting to help people. You can do it! You have a chance to rise up and be that person without having to worry about not having somebody having their back! I'm here and I know how you feel.

"We are imperfectly us. We are no longer an echo!"

I've always said this and I'm an advocate for helping people see that there IS a life after diagnosis. There is a way of moving forward and it starts with you. Accepting your disability and knowing that you're not alone is the first step.

I chose to be "Mrs Mindful". I chose to let myself show others that we can achieve things. I may have had a fantastic job before, but I wasn't really happy. I was living my life on autopilot.

Now, I cherish my days, whether in bed on lots of meds, house-bound I know I can help others and show them that we can achieve no matter what! Life is about the journey and enjoying it. My journey started and so can yours.

99

Break through those boundaries and chains and make your life change for the better.

Knowing that you are an amazing person, who can fulfil your dreams and have a great life that you want for your family so that it makes you feel like you can conquer anything in this world is important. Your disability will not define you unless you allow it to. Break through those boundaries and chains and make your life change for the better.

I am living proof that you can come through the other side and be smiling, even when living in pain daily. Even through the gap from diagnosis you can always reach out and know that you are not alone. This story I am sharing with you isn't just about me.... this is about everyone being a family and growing like the tree of life. I have never felt so grounded.

As I write this, I feel amazing because throughout school I was told I was not going to go anywhere in life! It's all happened since I've had to change my life due to my health. Life can throw curveballs and every day can be a challenge that you look into the eyes of and say; "I'm coming for you!", even with tears in your eyes. Diagnosis is the first day of the rest of your new life and it's one that you shouldn't shy away from. Moving forward and making your life better every single day by knowing that you can change lives with sharing your story, creating a business, showing others you will not be stopped. You can be a role model for many, and it starts with you saying 'yes'.

I am involved with a charity called Burning Nights CRPS (complex regional pain syndrome) and my ongoing advice and help to others about this topic, that isn't really spoke about in the mainstream, helps me to help them. I love my business and everything I have created since I was medically retired. I know I'm making a difference in the world and I'm excited for my future.

Dedication

I'm so thankful to my family and my wonderful sister who have been there for me always. I'm also grateful that I have the amazing support of my husband and I will always be ever thankful to him. To have these incredible people supporting me throughout my entire journey I know I am blessed.

Angie Candler

Angie Candler

Angie Candler has been married 3 years this year and she has a maine coon-cross-persian. She loves to cook and spend time with her family, as they are all very close. She lives in Hertfordshire with her hubby and kitty. Her daughter and granddaughter's live overseas.

She loves chatting to lots of friends and family online as that is her lifeline to the world.

She is currently creating "Beyond my Diagnosis" which is going to help a lot of people who suffer with pain and who feel as though they have been left behind in the world.

Angie is the Creator & CEO of her "Mrs Mindful" Company. She created it because she suffers from a lot of health issues that slowly made her look into every aspect of my life, especially as she has severe allergies that cause her to have anaphylactic shocks due to a lot of man-made ingredients. Angie also suffers from a rare condition called Erythiamy-algia (which has no cure), fibromyalgia, Lupus, Raynauds & Complex Regional Pain Syndrome. This is why the "Mrs Mindful" Range of amazing products was opened to the public.

"Mrs Mindful" offers a range of clean products to the public that are very affordable for you – as that was Angie's goal to make sure that the costs are kept down and making sure the product quality wasn't impacted.

"Mrs Mindful" shows the world that self-care isn't selfish & you shouldn't feel guilty! In this day and age, everyone needs to indulge in your self-care & stop rushing around at least once a day - whether it's for 5 minutes or an hour-long soak in the bath.

Angie's business is global and she's having fun with it all and loving the customer feedback.

WEB LINKS.

Website: www.mrsmindful.co.uk
Facebook Page: https://www.facebook.com/MrsMindful
Instagram: https://www.instagram.com/mrsmindfulcrew

99

Never give up, always get up."

ANESKA VERMAAK

Success happens when you believe

When I look back to when I started, I can see what I have gone through and to think from since I was little, I was always told I wouldn't make it.
What I'm doing will never be good enough.

My mother was and always will be my biggest fan and believer in all of my life.

One thing I can tell you from what I have gone through, and yes, I might only be 22yrs old, but I can tell a story that will bring tears to your eyes and you would wonder how I got through it. The biggest thing that I can tell you, as you are reading this, is that your story is there for you to write no one else.

I have been in the abusive relationship.
I have been through the break-up and the life of being cheated on.
I have been through fighting for my life and being told that I wouldn't make it. Seeing doctor after doctor that couldn't find what was wrong with me.

I was born premature at only 7 months, weighing in under 2kgs. My parents were given the news that if I survive the next 12hours I would be lucky. You see, my lungs hadn't developed, and I was hooked to machines in the Neo-Natal ICU ward. As the 12 hours passed, the doctors said; "let's see how the next 24 hours go". Well, as you can see, I made it and I know deep inside of me I was born to achieve great things.

> "you're not good enough for this job"
>
> ...
>
> "you don't qualify for this position" ...
> "you can't do that"...
> "this won't work"

We all face difficult times and my health is not the best, but I'm in control of how I live my life now. I'm in control to show people that it's possible to love the life you have been brought into. To love your body, to love yourself and to believe that you are the one that's going to create the story and make everyone realise that they are in control of making their own.

I have gone through being told... "you're not good enough for this job" ... "you don't qualify for this position" ... "you can't do that"... "this won't work" and honestly, I can tell you it eventually got to me.

I sat back and I just thought that maybe I'm not meant to be in this industry, maybe I'm not meant to make a change.

Have you ever felt this way, in your life? in your work? In your business?

Can you understand?

That's the thing - we are so quick to judge ourselves and not allow ourselves to see the beauty within us and see our own light that can shine on anyone to encourage and motivate them.

At a very young age I was told that I wouldn't see the rest of my life, because of my health issues and it shocked and upset me. When people tell you you're not going to live, in a health situation, to hear those actual words being said to you - it is much harder than someone telling you that you're not going to make it in a business situation or that something isn't going to work within your business or work position.

It is difficult to hear it, but one thing I can tell you is that you need one person. That one person who believes in everything about you. That will go against all odds to make you rise up and you have to find that person. For me, it was my mother.

It was my decision to prove everyone wrong that gave me only bad news. I want a life filled with positivity. Not only did I leave school and complete my studies. But when I did, I saw that there was no work available for me. (as most positions wanted experience of 2 to 3 years minimum).

How do you get the experience if you have just finished studies? I sent in my resume and was told the same thing time after time again - that knowledge was needed in the position's I had applied for.

Then one evening, not really knowing which way to turn and feeling a little defeated and despondent, I came across a social media advert about working from home via online sales and marketing.

Thinking to myself; "well I have nothing to lose", I sent a message. To which I received an immediate reply and then a telephone call. Feeling very excited after the call and thinking I can do this as I have nothing to lose and only to gain, I decided to join and do my best.

Well, it was not easy, and I had a lot to learn. Not being anything that I had ever studied before, this was all so brand new. Still determined to prove to everyone I could be a success, I gave it my all. This new start for me led me to a new opportunity, where I became the youngest person to achieve the Diamond rank and to launch the company in South Africa.

Now I felt empowered, and as though the sky was not even the limit.

Learning to deal with day-to-day issues which was a full mixture of clients, team members, product issues and imports, I learnt new skills as I was working my new business. With all this happening, I was able to buy my first house before I turned 20 years old. I was also able to travel to the UK and to Las Vegas as part of my business. Being able to connect with other successful entrepreneurs from all walks of life.

So, you may be thinking to yourself now, "well, this sounds fantastic, but can I do it"?

We all have the ability to achieve greater things in our lives, we just don't always focus on our own strengths and talents. Watching the famous people on television or super models and dreaming about a better life. Sitting wishing for it, won't help you achieve it. Each and every famous person started off battling and were even poor. Not knowing if tomorrow will be better, but no matter what, they kept fighting forward for the dream they had focused on.

One of the things that helped me was to write down goals. Goals that were easy to achieve. If you overwhelm yourself, you will give up. So, making goal posts daily that you can reach, will motivate you and empower you to set more goals and bigger goals.

As I am part of a generation of social marketing and being able to help others reach and find their potential in their lives. I am so grateful for the amazing opportunities that I have been able to enjoy.

> **"**
> **We all have the ability to achieve greater things in our lives, we just don't always focus on our own strengths and talents.**

Aneska Vermaak

Aneska Vermaak

Aneska Vermaak is a photographer and works in design. She is also a speaker and professional network marketer. Aneska lives in South Africa with her animals.

Between 2016 and 2019 she photographed Swan Lake Ballet and Beautiful Show. She was also an Obags Photographer and a Corner Coffee House Photographer.

In 2018 Aneska spoke at the James Yates' Event. Also in 2018, Aneska was announced as one of the Young Rising Stars in network Marketing after being the youngest ever to achieve the Diamond rank in the company she was involved in at the time.

In 2019 Aneska was offered 2 opportunities from Rebecca Adams. She flew from South Africa to the UK to be a Guest Speaker at Rebecca's Empowerment Convention IGNITE Live Event and was also featured and interviewed on the International Interview Series 2019.

Her hobbies are singing, painting, photography, walking her dogs, building relationships and travelling the world. Her mission is to inspire as many people worldwide as possible.

WEB LINKS.
Personal Facebook page: https://www.facebook.com/aneska.wide
Business Facebook page: https://www.facebook.com/awidephotography
Instagram: https://www.instagram.com/wide_photography
Website: https://www.aneskawide.com

99

Life is full of opportunities and sometimes they will terrify you, but you must push yourself out of your comfort zone."

LOUISE GRANT

Experiencing Grief at a Young age and how it impacted my life.

I had a life changing event happen in my life at the age of 11.
My foster Dad dropped dead in front of me from a massive heart attack.

Trying to process that grief at such a young age was difficult. I didn't have a lot of support and my foster Mum was heartbroken. She tried her best to support me, but this experience has left a mark on both our lives.

When the anniversary rolls around every year I still have flashbacks to that night. I had some counselling afterwards, but no one could really help. I felt from a young age I was a lost cause and was pretty sure I wouldn't live past my teens. I am now 32 and the following pages will show you how I coped with grief at a young age.

I had a pretty traumatic childhood that involved a lot of stuff that I won't get into in this chapter as this chapter is about grief. When I lost my foster dad, my world fell apart. I had only been placed with this foster family a year prior to his death and we were celebrating the year while on holiday in Scotland when he died. From that day onwards I had always said to myself I would never return to Scotland again, as I felt only bad things could come from returning to the country he died in. Unbeknownst to me, the Universe had other plans.

To be honest it has only been in recent years that I have realized the strength it took for me to deal with his death.

I was so young and naïve, but I was surrounded by love and support from so many different people. I had never experienced death before. I had experienced loss, but nothing ever prepares you to lose someone you love. To this day I still think about him.

I don't have any contact with any of his family, which is sad, and a year after his death, my foster Mum decided to stop fostering as she felt she hadn't been able to process her husband's death and give me the right environment to grow up in. It still hurts me that I no longer speak to anyone involved. I believe this has been the root cause of many of my adult mental health struggles.

I developed depression at the age of 14 and I ended up being assigned a community psychiatric nurse for the next 4 years. The reason I still talk about my foster Dad's death is because I feel it was a pivotal moment in my life that changed my whole outlook on life. I realized how precious life was but at the same time, I didn't want to live my life.

From the age of 14 I have made several suicide attempts and it has long continued into my adult life, my last attempt being a year ago.

After being diagnosed with emotionally unstable personality disorder at the age of 22, it took me several years, many psychiatric hospital admissions and years of psychology appointments to realize that my foster Dad's death had nothing to do with me. I don't really know why I blamed myself but deep down I wondered why such a good man had to die. I always felt I wasn't worthy of living and that is why I have tried so many times to end my life.

Obviously, there is a reason I am still here and writing this chapter today. Someone has always saved me from death - whether it be a partner, a professional, a friend or myself, there has always been that little ray of hope that has pulled me through my darkest days. I feel like I have a guardian angel watching over me.

My mental health journey started a few months after my foster Dad died. I can remember being in first year in high school and crouching in the corridor crying because I felt so overwhelmed. This happened most days and I would always be taken to the vice principal's office to recover from what I now know was panic attacks. This anxiety would stay with me all through my teenage years and all my adult life.

People always ask me; "How do you cope with such crippling anxiety?" My answer is always the same - music, meditation, deep breathing and distraction techniques.

It has been a long road, and only now 20 years later - Do I truly have control over my anxiety? Some days are better than others. The days that are better I feel like I can rule the world, but when the bad days come, I just want to isolate myself away from everyone and everything.

Anxiety is a journey that I wouldn't wish on anyone, but the good news is that there is support and help available. You are not alone.

People always ask me; "How do you cope with such crippling anxiety?"

First, you need to admit to yourself that the feelings or thoughts you are having are anxiety, but I would also recommend seeking a health professional's opinion as soon as you feel that you might have anxiety.

Anxiety has a lot of symptoms and can present in many ways. It isn't just a feeling. It can be irrational thoughts, and chest pains. It can be panic attacks and feeling like everything is too much or feeling extremely overwhelmed by things that don't seem to bother others. Anxiety is an illness and there are medications out there that will help control your symptoms. I know people can be wary about taking medication but trust me it is the one thing that keeps me sane. For years I was left unmedicated and those were the years that left the most scars on my life.

> **I had so many negative feelings that the outside world felt like a very frightening and overwhelming place to be.**

Every day I wonder if I had have realized what my symptoms were sooner, would I have had a completely different outlook on life?

Anxiety has ruled my life for so long, but three years ago I took a massive step in overcoming my anxiety by working one-on-one with a mental health support worker. By the time I had gotten to know my second support worker things had become so bad that I hadn't left the house alone in a year. I was diagnosed with agoraphobia and was put on medication to help me overcome my fear of the outside world. I had so many negative feelings that the outside world felt like a very frightening and overwhelming place to be.

Remember near the beginning of chapter I said that after my foster Dad died and that I never wanted to visit Scotland again? Well, six years ago my best friend committed suicide - which was another devastating blow. In the following months after her death I realized if I stayed in Northern Ireland that I was going to become another statistic.

On the 24th of November 2014, after 3 days of packing up my house, I got the first boat to Scotland and believe it or not, found a place in a homeless shelter in the town that my foster Dad had died in. I didn't realize this until about a month after I had arrived when I had yet again tried to take my own life.

I was in the local A and E department receiving treatment for an overdose. I left my cubicle in the A and E department and was standing looking at the signs that directed you to different areas of the hospital, when I had a feeling of déjà vu and I thought I have been here before. In my confusion I decided to take a walk and it was only when I got to the resus bays that it clicked in my brain that this is the hospital my foster Dad was pronounced dead in.

Still to this day I can remember the goosebumps and chills that came over me that evening and the feeling of dread that this was the hospital that I had ended up in. I felt like it was a sign that this wasn't the end of my journey. That I had a lot more to experience and live through.

I felt my foster Dad by my side that night and when the crisis team came to assess me, I blurted all this out to them. To be honest I think they thought I had officially lost my mind. They were support-ive but seemed a bit wary of my tale and told me it was the drugs I had overdosed on that had caused this reaction.

Deep down I knew that wasn't true. I can remember everything so clearly. I can remember walking into the resus bay to give my foster Dad a kiss goodbye and I can remember the yellow signs that were placed above the different areas of the emergency department.

The memories are all I am left with now, and at times, I wish I had kept in contact with his family. To them it was too painful to keep in contact with me but to me it felt like yet another abandonment and that the one thing that should have kept us together ripped us apart and left shells of the people we were. We bonded over such a tragic situation and now to think they no longer have a part in my life makes me incredibly sad.

There are days when I wonder what he would say to me. Would he be proud of the person I had become? or would he be telling me to make something of my life and to not let my anxiety win?

There are still days, especially around his anniversary, that I wonder if he hadn't have died how my life would have turned out. He was a role model to me and every year on his anniversary I send him a kiss and a hug up to heaven and tell him I love him.

In that one year we spent together he changed my life. He made me realize that in life sometimes you must go through your worst days and try to remember that better days are coming. In those deep dark depressions when it feels like there is no way out of the dark hole I have created, I always go back to that night and think of him. I think of all the people I know that have passed away, there have been many, and I realize this is all part of the plot.

Experiencing grief at that young age was heartbreaking but also eye opening. It made me realise that tomorrow is not promised to anyone and that sometimes you need to experience a traumatic event to show you how important living life to the full is.

To this day whenever I find myself in a dark place I try to remember that those dark places just need a little bit of light to show you the corners of the room so that you don't feel like that you are trapped and alone. That tiny shard of light can change your whole perspective.

I want you all to know that no matter how difficult your journey gets, that you are not on this journey alone. There are many other people out there facing the same problems that you have overcome, and that one day your story might inspire someone not to give up.

It might give them that much light of hope in the middle of the darkness.

Mental illness is still a taboo subject and people are scared to talk about it incase it turns in to an epidemic but my view is, if everyone talks about what they have experienced and how they have overcome those challenges, it might just give that hope to someone else who is maybe facing the same journey. I believe if you talk things through with someone, be it a friend, a partner or a professional, once you have got your thoughts out there your anxiety will start to calm down.

You have a story to tell and my advice is to get your story out there, whether it is through a journal, a blog, or writing a book, I can tell you now your story will inspire others. The universe will bring the right opportunities into your life at the right time.

I have always wanted to write a book as I feel my story would inspire many people, and then this opportunity landed in my life. It is an opportunity that I was guided to take and for once in my life I didn't ignore this prompting.

No matter what you believe in, if something comes along that resonates with your soul and your life goals, then no matter how scared you are, take that leap and learn how to do it later. Life is full of opportunities and sometimes they will terrify you, but you must push yourself out of your comfort zone.

> **Life is full of opportunities and sometimes they will terrify you, but you must push yourself out of your comfort zone.**

There are so many things that experiencing grief at a young age has taught me.

1. No matter what life throws at you, if you have support of family or friends, and you remember that the darkness doesn't last forever all you need it is that little spark of hope to light up the room.

2. Even though you have experienced such a traumatic experience it will teach you empathy and compassion and you will see the world from a different view like through a third person's perspective.

97

3. It has taught me that you learn who your true friends are.

I don't speak to anyone from my early teens, after I lost my foster Dad and I found it very hard to connect with peers or relatives on an emotional level. I was always classed as strange and different by people my own age and they found they couldn't relate to me or my circumstances which only made my depression and mental health a lot harder to deal with. During my teens I felt like I was fighting a losing battle and every day felt a struggle from dealing with daily worries and also the harder stuff I had to deal with like my own past. I always felt like an alien from a different world. I never felt like I belonged and for much of my adult life I have felt the same.

Now I have a lot of support from my local mental health team and the amazing facilities in my local area. I finally feel like I am at the stage of my life that I can finally say my mental health is better than it has ever been, and that after my many years of struggling, my anxiety and depression seem to be getting easier. I do still have my bad days, but everyone struggles occasionally. For me my episodes have been becoming a lot less frequent and I feel they are completely different to what they were like during my earlier years and I do believe it is because of all the help and support that I now have.

Four years ago, I met my husband and he has helped me so much over the years. This year we celebrate 3 years of marriage and to be honest, this relationship has totally surprised me as I had never seen myself settling down as I found trusting people so difficult.

My husband is my rock and without him I wouldn't be the person I am today. He deserves to have the last few sentences of my chapter.

Louise Grant

Louise Grant

Louise Grant was born in Belfast and moved to Scotland six years ago.

She found her soulmate in 2016 and they have been married 3 years this year. Louise is a fur mama and avid crocheter. She enjoys nothing more than sitting down with my latest crochet project and listening to music. She loves most music, but her favourite genre is Country.

Louise loves all things Disney and her favourite movie is Mary Poppins. She loves the fact that Disney are remaking all the old classics into live action movies.

Louise is currently working towards becoming a Cognitive Behaviour therapist, and this year she has completed an online employability course. She loves to learn new things, and she is constantly looking to expand her knowledge. She is invested in working on her mindset and becoming more positive.

SOCIAL MEDIA LINKS.

Facebook: https://www.facebook.com/louise.adair.940

99

Knowledge is powerful.
Learn something every day."

RACHEL ALLASTON

I wish he had just hit me

Sounds daft wishing that doesn't it?
But when you think of Domestic Abuse you pre-
dominantly think of violence.
But it's the emotional and psychological abuse
that is harder to see and, to me,
harder to deal with.

If he had hit me then I would've had something
physical, tangible to get rid of him.
But he never did although he tried to goad me
into hitting him several times.

Everything I write about is purely my own experiences and thoughts and some may find familiarity in it and some may think I'm being over-dramatic about it. Nevertheless, this is my story. .

When I first met him, I was going through a particularly bad time in life. I was very low in myself; I don't believe I was suffering from depression, but I was definitely heading that way, and I came across him online. He seemed to be everything I was looking for. He was saying all the right things to make me believe he was a hardworking family man and that all he wanted was to take care of us. I had a daughter from a previous relationship with special needs.

In the beginning he was very adamant about being punctual with phone calls etc. If I was only a few minutes late he would start messaging me saying that I was ignoring him and not interested, he had me apologising and trying to placate him from the word go! How I didn't see it and I put up with that behaviour is baffling to me. I had never ever thought I would be that type of person!

> **How I didn't see it and I put up with that behaviour is baffling to me. I had never ever thought I would be that type of person!**

It didn't take long before he had met my daughter and had her wrapped around his little finger. She loves everyone and he glorified in her affection for him. He also had a daughter whom he was fighting through the courts to gain access to. He sang a sob story that was worthy of an Oscar, he was the abuse victim, he was physically beaten by his ex and she had him arrested when he had done nothing wrong blah blah blah... It should've been one of things I questioned more but I believed him when he was crying over it all. Little did I know they were crocodile tears.

Throughout the court process I helped him with everything, filling in applications etc including a letter of support from me. And he won! By the time he had access to his daughter, I was already pregnant with our first child together, a boy. He was not happy about that!

In fact, the sonographer actually asked if everything was alright as he looked so furious about it! I don't know why he was so determined to have all girls but apparently it was my fault it was a boy!

During the pregnancy he decided to do some work on the house and as work was slowing down at the agency he was employed through, he took some time off to get treatment for the health conditions he has. So, we made a claim for benefits and everything went in my name. He didn't want anything in his name. He didn't even like having to pay for anything on a card or online! He would usually give his mum the cash and have her pay for things – strange!

By the time I was due to give birth, his depression started to show. He had thrown my cats out even though they had only ever been indoors, my boy has since disappeared but 4 years later and my girl is starting to finally be happy in the house again.

He would get so down and claim it was about his daughter. He always wanted to know how much money was in my account as I had full 'control' of all the money – no he just didn't want anything in his name so his ex could apparently take it! Hmmm not sure I ever really believed that one.

When I had my eldest boy it was a bit of an ordeal, it took them 5 days to get me induced. I was so tired, and he insisted on staying with me, which was fine except he smoked like a chimney and would want money for cigarettes, didn't care about personal hygiene, totally gross!

But my son eventually arrived, and he instantly declared he looked exactly like his daughter and therefore just like him. He didn't, he looked exactly like my daughter and still does! Everyone said how alike they are which used to really annoy him, and he would get really moody. When he was like that, we literally walked on eggshells around him. He never got physical, but he would just made snide comments and digs at us, proclaim he was the head of the household and what he said goes.

With our boy, however, he never ever put him down, literally never! He was love bombing and he would actually give me dirty looks and leave the room if I was feeding him. He hated that I was breastfeeding and the day he turned 4 months old he decided he was going to start weaning him and give him a bottle. I was not happy but unless I got into a physical altercation, which he tried to goad me into, there was nothing that was going to stop him.

All of this just sounds like he was a bit of a twat but during this time he further separated me from friends, he would insist on doing the school runs telling people I was resting, making himself out to be partner of the year!

There had apparently been an incident where my mum was rude to his family, which they denied, but he insisted it was true so from then on he declared my family were rude, disgusting, dirty and he said I was never to take HIS son to see them. I did but he would insist on coming too and would look down his nose at them and act like they were living in a plague infested hovel!

It used to annoy me so badly, but I would send pictures and make excuses as to why we couldn't go see them and they couldn't come to us, not that they liked to. It was so embarrassing as he would make it obvious that he didn't want them there and he would be clattering around in the kitchen making as much noise as possible. Basically, being a complete twat!

Eventually I was getting torn in two as he wouldn't go to their house and they wouldn't come to our house. However, his family we saw every week! They were welcome whenever they wanted! It was so frustrating, but I kept myself quiet, so I didn't annoy him because living with him in a mood was indescribable. He didn't really do or say anything but the atmosphere! Shocking! You didn't dare upset him further and to this day I never know why I felt that way.

When my eldest was approx 4 months old I fell pregnant again. I believed as I was exclusively breastfeeding I was safe and he had been 'monitoring' me for when he could have sex again. That was when the nagging and whinging began about his 'needs' as a man!

I eventually gave in just to shut him up and he didn't care about me at all. His sole focus was his gratification and impregnating me again, which happened so quickly I was shocked! And he did that more than once, several times in fact.

Anyway, the day I took the pregnancy test and it showed up positive there was no reaction at all from him. He just looked at me and said 2 things – at least it will be here before the tax credits cut off and it had better be a girl this time. I just sat on the toilet and cried, he had already gone and left me alone - I just cried. I admit I was torn about whether I wanted this baby or not, I would feel guilty for thinking it wouldn't be bad thing if I had a miscarriage than bring another baby into this environment.

However, the baby grew strong and healthy and then we went for the scan. It was another boy. He was so angry! The poor sonographer didn't know what to do. It was so obvious she was disturbed by his reaction and I tried to make light of it and make a joke, but you could cut the atmosphere with a knife. She was very professional, but she was clearly hurrying up to get my scan over with. I just felt like crying, I blamed it on hormones. A lot got blamed on hor-mones!

> **I just cried. I admit I was torn about whether I wanted this baby or not, I would feel guilty for thinking it wouldn't be a bad thing**

After this was when his mental health started to take a serious decline. He was being increasingly controlling over things like my appearance. He would say I should care about, what he thinks given he's my partner and father of my kids. He would be monitoring the traffic going past the house, observing if a particular car had gone past too often for his liking. He would stand out at the front of our house smoking, glowering at everyone that went past. He was verbally abusive to my elderly neighbours who had been so lovely to me and my daughter. They didn't say a word to me after that. However, we now have a lovely relationship thank goodness.

A few days before my due date we had an almighty argument and this time I grabbed my son (my daughter was at her dads) and I took off to my mums. My sister had said that our sister who lives in the USA had sent over some goodies and I went to collect them. The argument was about me not taking my boy with me to collect the stuff as I was 'banned' from taking him there! So I got there and I soon as I saw my sister I started ranting about what an idiot he was and that I wanted to leave him, but I didn't know how to get him out of my house without it impacting his daughter's court arrangement – not that it did in the end anyway!

> **I was playing down making out it wasn't as bad as it seemed but yet I would message her about him but would play it down later on.**

When my sister and one of my nephews suddenly appeared out of the kitchen! They had surprised me! My sister was that concerned for me she had flown over from America to see for herself what the hell was going on! She was hearing things from my sister which I was playing down making out it wasn't as bad as it seemed but yet I would message her about him but would play it down later on.

She came over to the house to meet him (just her and my nephew though, the others weren't welcome) and he put on his best show for her, trying to justify his behaviour towards the rest of my family. She just listened to him and didn't really make too many comments, just tried to make him see he wasn't really being fair, but he wasn't having any of it.

And I never know what exactly was said but he drove her back by himself and they ended up having an argument and he took off, tyres practically screeching when she had gotten out of the car. And that was everything negative she had heard about him proven, in one car ride.

110

When I went into hospital to have my son, everything went ok until the delivery and he was born very fast. The poor boy blew up like a purple plum and his eyes haemorrhaged. He looked like a little vampire with no white in his eyes at all, they were completely red! We were kept in because of my blood pressure but then he developed an infection in his cord.

My sister was still in the country but was due to leave the day after he was born. She had intended to come see us but woke up with a cold and didn't want to pass it on, so she never got to meet him. My mum came up to visit instead as he wasn't there or due to visit. He was not happy when he found out but calmed himself down by knowing my youngest sister didn't come. He hated her with a passion because she stood up to him. But while I was in hospital, I had to video call him every night even though I was having to go to the Neonatal intensive care unit every 4 hours and I wanted to sleep.

After a week I came home and the next day he started having a breakdown. He was massively paranoid. He would try to get out of the house to confront people. He would tell me to get off the internet because we were being monitored. He would spend all night pacing the back garden, chain smoking and lived on cups of tea. I got him to the local hospital and in front of the mental health team who referred him and gave him anti-depressants.

Day 7 - I found him showering himself down fully clothed in the bath. He admitted he had taken a massive overdose, but it hadn't worked other than to make his body release itself. That was the first time he was taken out by ambulance in front of the kids. The hospital decided to release him into my care even though he had had a psychotic breakdown! So now I had a disabled child, a 14 month old child, and a 2 week old baby, plus him to take care of. For about 2 weeks we lived in hell. The kids couldn't make a sound, no one was to watch the TV unless he did.

My eldest boy annoyed him one time and threw him across the room and he threatened to punch my daughter in her 'smug bitch' face!

That was it – he needed to leave. I needed a break!!!

We had a massive argument and I left with the kids to go for a walk and he messaged me to not come home yet. I discovered that he had taken another overdose. He told me if I ever dared to try to leave him or take his kids away, he would do it again and it would be all my fault.

That was it, he got taken out by ambulance again and this time I told him he had to go or I would call the police and have him removed. He did actually go this time after begging me not to do this and if it weren't for my family being so evil, I wouldn't be so cruel to him. I had no sympathy by that point and actually began to despise him.

The moment he was gone it was like a cloud had lifted! I immediately put the kids' TV programmes on loudly and we danced around and ordered in a pizza (we didn't do that before because he didn't like it). We were all so joyful he had gone. The intense feelings of guilt that rushed over me that the kids were so obviously happy the moment he was gone were almost unbearable. I had put them through that for so long and I was determined they would never ever feel like that again.

I now know all the signs were there, I just didn't see them. The different types of abuse he inflicted; I didn't realise.

However, we are now free. We are happy. We are safe. And that is everything.

I dedicate my chapter to my children -
Eleanor, Andrew and Daniel. I will never let anyone attempt to break you again. You are my world and I will never stop making you proud of your mama as I'm so proud of you.

Smashing Through the Glass Ceiling!

Rachel Allaston

Rachel Allaston

Rachel is from West Sussex and is a mum of 3.

Her eldest, a daughter, has a rare genetic condition which is degenerative. She also has 2 very energetic boys.

She is currently studying with the intent to not only to provide for her children but to also set an example to them that you keep on trying no matter what life throws at you.

She's a firm believer that knowledge is power.

SOCIAL MEDIA LINKS.

Instagram: https://www.instagram.com/thegingerwheelerandfamily

Facebook: https://www.facebook.com/rachel.allaston

99

Obstacles, problems or challenges are all part of the process, chiselling out the best in us as we move towards our goals."

Imani Speaks

Overcoming Obstacles

How Post-Natal Depression Led Me To Personal Development & Spiritual Growth

After I gave birth to my daughter Antoinette,
I suffered from terrible post-natal depression.
I just felt sad and would find myself crying
uncontrollably unable to stop.
I remember one day my mum came to visit us
and I burst into floods of tears and could not stop crying.
I really felt helpless and hopeless.

I was happy being a mother, but just felt empty and sad inside.

When Antoinette was two years old, I had found a part-time nursery for her which enabled me to get out of the house and a chance for her to make new friends. One day, as I was dropping Antoinette off, I noticed a little book shop across the road. I had been praying for my life to change and hadn't noticed the little book shop until now. I have always loved books, so couldn't wait to go in and see what books were available.

I had been brought up in a Christian home. My wonderful Gran had taught me how to read from the bible from a very early age. I had also studied Religious Education at school, so was familiar with religious text; but the books in the bookshop were not religious – they were metaphysical or spiritual. The difference to me is that religion focuses on dogma - the external, whilst spiritual growth is all about your own inner wisdom or your relationship with the source of all creation.

> **If I didn't like my life, I had the power to change it.**

My first Personal Development encounter was with books such as 'You Can Heal Your Life' by Louise L Hay and 'Creative Visualisation' by Shakti Gawain.

I would look forward to going to this magical bookshop finding new books that would open me up to my soul's purpose as I was fascinated, learning about the power of the mind and spiritual growth. I learned that I could change my life and make things happen; I didn't have to go through life being at the mercy of circumstances. If I didn't like my life, I had the power to change it. Reading these books transformed my way of thinking and helped me manage my post-natal depression and low self-esteem.

I went from feeling sad and empty, not wanting to get out of bed to being excited to wake up early and excited about the new day ahead. I learned about goal setting, visualization and changing my self-talk and limiting beliefs which really helped me to raise my vibration enabling me to manifest a new way of being.

HOW I WENT FROM OVERCOMING A FIRE DISASTER TO BECOMING A HAIR EXTENSION MASTER

I couldn't believe it when I looked in the mirror, the skin on my face, especially on my nose, had completely peeled off. I hadn't realised just how bad it was...

Earlier that day, I was getting myself and my little girl Antoinette ready to get her hair braided at the hairstylist. I was ringing the local mini-cab service to book a cab, when I heard an almighty explosion. The windows in my flat had jutted out of their panel and the walls were black.

I was so shocked and obviously worried about little Antoinette, who had been running around the flat, but thank God, she was completely unharmed.

I didn't realise that I was burning up and that the skin on my face was peeling off especially on my nose. As I touched my face, it would peel off in my hands and the skin on my nose had completely melted off. I was not looking good at all. I knew that I had to get to the hospital and find out the extent of my injuries. The cab came and we made a detour to the hospital.

What caused the explosion?
My central heating wasn't working at the time and it would take a couple of days before I could have it repaired, so I borrowed a fan-heater from a friend. While I was busy ringing 'round for a cab, little Antoinette who was getting a bit bored had been running around in and out of the living room and had got hold of an aerosol can which had rolled towards the fan-heater which had subsequently caused the explosion. We were lucky to be alive, considering what had happened.

This was back in the 1980's, before phone cameras and social media, so I have no photos, in fact, I could not bear to see myself in the mirror; especially during the weeks ahead as I was going through the healing process. The skin on my face was crusting and falling off and I was still experiencing some pain, but still, I was grateful to be alive and more importantly that Antoinette was unharmed.
I spent many nights crying and wondering whether I would recover from my injuries and would my skin ever return to normal.

Growing up, my gran and my mother would always say that nothing is all bad, something good always comes out of every bad experience. We just need to look for the good and not get stuck on the problem.

Back then, I had always struggled to do braids on my daughter's hair and on my own hair, so I took the easy way out and would go to the hairstylist whenever we wanted to have our hair braided. The stylist would always do a great job, but it was quite costly, and she lived on the other side of town.

At the time of my injury, I was working as a hospital secretary, so had to stay off work for a while. I had a lot of time on my hands, so I had time to practice hair-braiding with extensions. I eventually mastered my craft and was able to braid my daughter's hair as well as doing my own hair.

One day, my partner's work colleague asked if he knew anyone who could do the Bo Derek hairstyle. His girlfriend was travelling back to her native country Denmark and wanted a new look.
My partner came home that night excited about his conversation with his workmate and broke the news to me that he had booked me to braid the hair of my first paying client. I was really nervous and scared, but he reassured me that he knew I could do it, I wasn't so sure, but I took a leap of faith and said I would give it a go.

Wow, I did it! My first paying client, she was really happy with the hairstyle and even sent me a photo as promised and shared how she had received many compliments from friends and family.
I was motivated and inspired to start my own hair business and decided to advertise in "Black Hair and Beauty", a popular hair and beauty magazine at the time. I designed the advert using the photo that she sent me together with a photo of my sister Rosy.

My little business started off at a nice steady pace, I had a couple of clients here and there. I was still doing my day job, but as the weeks and months went by, I got more and more bookings. I could not keep up with the number of clients I was getting, so I had to bring my sister on board.

My sister Rosy and I couldn't keep up with what we called 'hair-jobs.' By now I had given up my day job and was doing hair-jobs full time. Things got so busy; we had to bring in my sister-in-law Bev.

Hair-jobs kept us all really busy and changed all of our lives financially and I also found that it's true - that people talk to their hairstylist about anything. So, I was able to share some of what I was learning from my own spiritual growth, which they seemed to appreciate.

I tell this story, to show that you can get through anything and have more, be more and do more than you did before.

While I was struggling with my burns and in pain, I would visualize seeing the skin on my face starting to heal and returning to normal. I would write out my goals and the things I wanted to manifest. I would listen to hours of personal development cassette recordings while practising my braiding skills.

I was a young woman in my mid-twenties during the eighties who had gone through a horrible

> I would visualize seeing the skin on my face starting to heal and returning to normal.

ordeal, but I refused to feel sorry for myself sitting around doing nothing. I decided that I would take action. I would learn something new that would take my mind off my ordeal and the pain I was experiencing and focused on what I can do right now.

No matter how bad it gets, you can always find the good and run with it. I was solution focused not problem focused.

The fire ordeal I went through meant I had to stay at home. Staying at home didn't mean being passive; it meant I could get active and learn something new. In the end, acquiring this new skill enabled me to work from home, working around my daughter, which meant that I could give up my day job and create a job of my own.

FAITH MIRANDA CAN'T SPEAK TO IMANI SPEAKS

Broadcasting on the radio was the last thing on my mind when my brother Carl called to have our usual chitchat about this and that. He was really excited about the various projects that had come his way after the success of his first book.

The opportunity to broadcast on the radio came to me when my life was at a standstill. At that time, I had stopped reading my personal development books, wasn't really setting goals or visualizing and was in a really low place. I was having marital problems and just feeling unfulfilled and in a stuck place.

The day my brother called, I was feeling particularly out of sorts and I had noisy repetitive negative thoughts in my head. My life, at that time, felt really predictable like having a 'ground hog day' experience.

That telephone call from Carl was about to change my life.

YES, YOU CAN!

Carl had written a book about his own struggles growing up with learning difficulties. The book had really taken off for him and I was proud of him and all that he was achieving. We were having our usual chats when he told me that he had been offered his own radio show. I was really excited for him.

Carl knew that I had always been a personal development enthusiast, but also that I was shy and very much a background person with low self-esteem, who wasn't utilising my gifts to the full extent. He was about to blast me out of my comfort zone!

He said, 'I've been offered a radio show, but I can't do it right now as I'm really busy with other projects, but I know someone who can, (drum roll) that person is 'YOU' and I've told the manager all about you and he's expecting your call.'

At that point, I bolted out of my chair. I kept saying 'no I can't,' but Carl was strong and focused and would not listen to my limiting beliefs and simply kept saying 'YES, YOU CAN!'

The next day, I called the radio station and arranged to meet for an interview with the radio owner - Minty. I remember my first day, Wednesday, 8 May 2013 (two days before my birthday). I was really nervous but knew I had to do it; I did not want to let Carl nor Minty down. I was here now, so I might as well give it a go.

Just as we were about to go live on the air Minty asked 'what are you going to call your radio show – what's your show's name?'. I hadn't thought of a name for my show and only had seconds to decide. My mouth opened and I heard myself saying 'Imani Speaks.' Imani means 'Faith' (Faith is actually one of my names) and Speaks because I had always struggled to find my voice and needed to listen to and trust my inner voice or intuition.

> I had always struggled to find my voice and needed to listen to and trust my inner voice or intuition.

I really had no time to think of a name, it was literally seconds before we went live. The name came to me in that moment and has stayed with me ever since.

I got through my first week and thought, 'okay, I think I can do this'. During the week, I got a call from Minty, 'You will be interviewing your first guest,' he obviously was joking, or I heard him wrong, 'my first what?' I asked, to which he repeated, 'you will be interviewing your first guest on your next show, he's a great guy you'll be alright.'

'Is he having a laugh?', I thought. I reluctantly agreed. It meant I would have a guest in the studio with me and I was going to ask questions and have to do it all live. I was just getting comfortable and now I was scared and nervous all over again. I asked for the guy's details, got in touch and Malik was so lovely, really reassured me that I had nothing to fear. We did the show and after that I was hooked on interviewing guests.

When I took on doing the radio show, I was planning to play music and in between do some small talk around personal development and personal growth. It has been seven years since my first broadcast; I've interviewed some of the most awe-inspiring people and have enjoyed some of the most life-changing conversations that have been mind shifting. I have had hundreds of conversations with people from all different walks of life, but all have delivered amazing insights into life's journey.

> ,,
> I was just getting comfortable and now I was scared and nervous all over again.

When my brother Carl approached me, I was shrinking back in life. At the time, I felt that I had lost myself in my marriage, supporting my husband's goals and not really thinking about what I wanted, who I was becoming. I had given up on my dreams.

Carl speaking with me that day, pouring positive nutritious words into my dormant spirit, not taking no for an answer, re-awakened something in me that led me to pick up the phone and call Minty. I was scared, but curious, why had this opportunity come to me and could I really do it?

I chose to share these three stories because all three have shaped my life in some way. They have all got me to crawl from out of my comfort zone, face my demons and go towards the light.

Smashing Through the Glass Ceiling!

You may be going through some tough times right now, maybe you feel lost, not sure what to do. You may feel as if someone else has taken the steering wheel of your life and that you are now in the passenger seat watching your life go by.
My message to you is that there is greatness within you, something magical that only you can do; only you can access. Others can point you to look within, but only you can enter that secret place where all that you need exists.

I invite you to go within to that secret place and there you'll discover the next new soul adventure of your life.

In memory of my Gran and my niece Selina and also to my Mum & Dad

Imani Speaks

Imani Speaks

Imani Speaks is a Radio Present & DJ, a Podcaster, Spiritual Coach, Poet & Lyricist, Co-Author, YouTube Vlogger and Speaker.

Imani has been a Spiritual Coach since 2004 and offers intuitive support to those who need to unpack emotional pain (in a safe space), particularly in the area of love and relationship.

The Imani Speaks Show and Podcast brings you interviews and conversations with talented musicians, authors, thought leaders, transformational coaches, business coaches and other community angels who are making a difference locally and globally.

Imani is also, not only an author in this book, but is working on a solo book project about the Journey of The Soul. She collaborates with singers and musicians for her poetry and lyrics and also blogs for online media organisations primarily around the areas of spirituality, personal development, love and relationships.

WEB LINKS.

Radio: www.conciousradio.com
Website is under construction.

Facebook: https://www.facebook.com/imanimedia

Soundcloud: https://soundcloud.com/imani-speaks

LinkedIn: https://uk.linkedin.com/in/imani-speaks-753927a6

Pinterest: https://uk.pinterest.com/imanispeaks1/boards/

Instagram: https://www.instagram.com/imanispeaks1/

99

Daunting as it may seem, take a deep breath and one step at a time, together we can do this!"

JILLY ASHWORTH

Who'd have thought...

It was not quite how I imagined my visit with Andy to be, who had undergone an operation to remove more of his leg and was up on the ward recuperating, or so I thought.

There I was, standing in the queue at Costa - there's always a queue at the hospital Costa – when my phone buzzed. I saw the hospital number displayed on the screen and my stomach dropped. I knew something had gone awry but, as to what, I wasn't sure. I was asked to go to the Adult Intensive Care Unit where a doctor would meet me.

Deserting the queue, I speedily made my way up to the AICU. My heart was beating 19 to the dozen and after being beeped in I was taken to Andy. I'd never been in the AICU before and as I passed the many patients lying in their beds, with tubes and wires everywhere, I could feel my heart begin to pick up the pace even more.

The shock of seeing Andy hooked up to several machines with a tube down his throat and unconscious was tenfold. His doctor was trying to explain something to me, but I couldn't understand or comprehend what he was saying. "Is he in a coma?" I questioned. Again, the doctor started to explain using medical language, but I still couldn't focus on what he was trying to tell me.

I eventually calmed down enough to ask him to explain what had happened again. The gist of it was that Andy had arrested on the operating table and had to be injected with adrenaline to get his heart to start pumping again. His lungs had filled with fluid because one of his valves wasn't working correctly and wasn't stopping the back-flow properly. His lungs weren't working on their own so the medical team sedated him and a breathing tube was inserted. The doctor, on leaving, advised me that the cardiologist would be popping down to speak to me.

> **His lungs weren't working on their own so the medical team sedated him and a breathing tube was inserted.**

Left on my own, I approached Andy, trying to take it all in. Monitors were beeping, the machine helping him breathe was pumping repetitively and a nurse stood in the corner of the room keeping an eye on everything. Stupid things went through my mind; his brother was on holiday... should I bother him? His mother lives in Kent and I knew I would need to tell her but could I do it without breaking-down? Did that even matter? I should ring work, I couldn't possibly go in and leave him on his own. I need to tell the boys. Who should I phone first?

I honestly can't remember in which order I did phone the family; but I think it was his brother. I asked him to ring his mum for me and tell her that I would call her later. My son, Zac, still recalls me phoning him saying, "You need to sit down," at which point he just told me to get on with it (they weren't his actual words), the worst already zooming around in his mind and heaviness pulling him down. To say I'm not good in a crisis....

Norma, Andy's mum, arrived the following day. She was 78 at the time, but thought nothing of travelling half-way across London to get on a train and head up to Nottingham to be with her boy. Her anguish was obvious and after asking a lot of questions, she just sat there holding his hand or stroking his arm.

We were told not to expect anything to happen that day, however, they said they would try and bring him off the ventilator after 48 hours. Norma and I visited on that Friday where, eventually, they decreased the amount of sedative to bring him slowly round. Relief surged through me as Andy gradually began to show signs of it wearing off. He started to claw at the tube still inserted into his throat with panic and fear in his eyes. He obviously couldn't understand what was happening, but we kept talking to him, saying he must leave it in as they needed to make sure he could breathe on his own. After a few agonising minutes, the doctors decided that all was good and removed the tube. Andy started to try to speak but not much made sense at this stage. Eventually it became clear that he was asking what had happened. We told him, but I know he didn't take it in at that time.

Norma and I visited again the following day. Andy was more alert and trying to crack jokes (never one to miss an opportunity) and, since waking, his claim to fame is that he 'died' for three minutes...

We did find humour in those dark days when everything felt incredibly hard, frustrating and Andy feeling so low that he often thought that he didn't want to 'live like this'. His medication happened to leave one particular side effect. He was given furosemide to combat the water retention he was experiencing. Of course, being horizontal, meant that the water retention found a particularly embarrassing area to visit. Cantaloupe melons was my reaction, the doctor's being "they're impressive." Needless to say, Andy was very uncomfortable in more ways than one.

As part of my role as a teaching assistant, I am often asked to go on residentials with the year group I am working with. As it happened, I was working with Year 5 and their trip was to PGL (Peter Gordon Lawrence – aka "Parents Get Lost") Activity Centre near Lincoln. This had been arranged for many months and was due to take place on 28 March 2018, for two nights. The staff at the hospital didn't think that Andy would be released before then because of the medication he was receiving for his heart, and the recovery of his stump.

I had only missed visiting Andy on three occasions, due to extreme weather conditions (snow) and thought this would be an ideal time to just do something different, something for me. Of course Andy had other ideas and by the time this trip arrived he'd had enough and thought it would be a fabulous idea to get himself discharged, even with knowing that I wasn't going to be at home to help him. I don't know what he thought he could do by himself but there you go, not stubborn much.

He rang me on my first evening to say that he was being transported home the next day. I couldn't believe it. I asked him to wait until I was home but would he? No way! He just couldn't stay another day. Staying in hospital is never fun, but to spend just under three months in one hospital or another is enough to make anyone lose it.

I offered to come home that night, but he said not to and that he could manage with the help of the boys. I took him at his word and stayed. Orders were given to the boys – I'd done nothing about the sleeping arrangements – that they should move the furniture around in the living room and take our bed downstairs. I could hear the silent groans down the phone but they got on with it. Andy was transferred by ambulance and helped into the house and settled on the bed. (When Andy had his left leg amputated in the May of 2016, we thought that was hard enough; but two legs?}

Arriving home after PGL, of course I was eager to see how Andy was getting on. Apparently, it had been a tough night on all the boys as the medication Andy was taking was playing havoc with his digestive system. Unable to get out of bed quickly - well, not at all - a bedpan was required. Andy had probably hoped that none of the boys would ever get to see such a thing, never mind actually having to take care of the issue. I think the boys have been scarred for life and were more than happy to pass on the baton.

Andy remained bed-bound for some time afterwards, learning how to sit up etc. It was incredibly hard and frustrating for both of us. We remained sleeping in the living room up until December that year. Andy's mum kindly gave us the means to have our bedroom extended so that Andy could have easy access to space and a bigger en-suite. We will forever be grateful to her for that, otherwise Andy may not have showered at all in the last two years. Andy has his prosthetics now but is still mainly wheelchair-bound.

The stressful layers of the last four years finally took their toll on me. I was signed off work to help Andy cope for a month or two. During this time, I'd been getting twinges in my coccyx area followed by being diagnosed with both golfer's elbow and tennis elbow. Ridiculous really as I've very rarely played either...

However, after eight months or so of suffering, I noticed that my hips and neck hurt, as did various other parts of my anatomy. If I stood or sat too long, I would find that when I moved the pain became acute and would only fade if I stretched or walked it out (very slowly). The doctor thought I may be vitamin D deficient and did that blood test, along with several others. There were various markers which meant my bone density was borderline and I was borderline arthritic but, before they took that any further, they asked me to take a course of vitamin D as my numbers were low. Apparently, having aches and pains in your legs can be an indication that you are vitamin D deficient.

> **Andy remained bed-bound for some time afterwards, learning how to sit up etc. It was incredibly hard and frustrating for both of us.**

After 6-8 weeks, however, there was no improvement and so I was referred to Kings Mill where I met with a consultant who, after a physical exam and lots of questioning, informed me that I had fibromyalgia. I'd done a bit of research into this and wasn't exactly surprised. At least it wasn't rheumatoid arthritis, they said, which apparently is worse, although, having fibromyalgia, I'm not actually sure that's true. Fibromyalgia is a condition that affects the soft and fibrous tissues throughout the body and is often brought on by stress. It causes the brain to misinterpret what the body is saying and sends signals to say it's in pain. It feels a bit like having boxed ten rounds with Joe Bugner (although Andy says I should say a more recent boxer's name but, for the life of me, I can never remember one).

And that's another thing – brain fog – known as 'fibro-fog'. It is a bit like having a 'baby brain'. I have difficulty in thinking of appropriate words or even sentences. A sufferer of fibromyalgia can also have increased sensitivity to pain, extreme tiredness (fatigue), muscle stiffness, difficulty sleeping (oh yes, since having fibro I've started snoring too - so Andy says anyway), headaches and irritable bowel syndrome. It's not fun.

Like any invisible disability many people just don't know what I'm dealing with, some of whom think I'm after the sympathy vote and say things like, "Oh it's just your age, you're getting old". Not me; I'm a grafter, I was brought up knowing that if you want to get anywhere in life you have to work at it, nobody's going to do it for you.

> ❝
> ## Like any invisible disability many people just don't know what I'm dealing with

So, you can imagine the frustration of not being able to do some of the simplest chores and having to ask for others to help. Anybody who knows me knows that I rarely ask for help and will usually just get on with whatever needs doing. Thinking about it, this was probably more than inevitable.

Over the last four years I've suffered a mini breakdown, helped one of my children get back on the straight and narrow after he took an overdose and, while in Majorca on holiday with family and friends, I was crushed between a car and a wall. While loading the boot with shopping, Laura started the car to get the air-con working not realising it was in reverse gear. The car jumped backwards knocking me into the wall behind it. My god that hurt. I couldn't feel my legs as the bumper had rammed me into the wall with some force. We managed to get help from passers-by and an ambulance was dispatched. Laura rang Andy saying, "I think I've broken your wife." Happy Birthday Andy!

In May 2016, Andy had his left leg amputated and, after a week of him being at home, my father died suddenly of a heart attack. People say things happen in threes but I think we had double whammy. Also, our youngest child, Will, has also paid the price and often blames himself for not having seen the signs of how poorly his dad was. We often talk to him about this, saying that the professionals took three days to work out that he should be in A&E as he had sepsis and that there was nothing he could have done but he still carries that burden. He receives counselling and will often go and talk to his pastoral support teacher, who has been absolutely amazing. Andy often jokes (I hope), "What have you got to be stressed about?"

Even though Andy has become a lot more independent he is still very reliant on others, usually me. My daily weekday routine starts at 6.15am. I give him his wash stuff (which he uses while lying in bed; it's easier) including a towel, his underwear and his gel stock for his leg. While he's doing this I will go downstairs and make a cup of coffee, set out his clothes for the day, put out his breakfast if he's having any, only to jump back in bed with my coffee for the time it takes him to eat breakfast etc. I'll then help him into his suit and assist him into the car. Andy has hand controls to enable him to drive.

When he comes home I do the reverse and help him change into comfortable clothing, get him a drink and start dinner. Andy can do these things for himself, but it takes him ten times longer than it does me. At least he's up and about and off to work, which is very important for his mental health. It's amazing how far he's come. He uses walking sticks to walk to and from the car. However, just recently, he has learnt the best way to remove the wheelchair from the car and put it back in by himself without falling over!

If it wasn't for the generosity of Andy's family, we could also have been facing having to move from our house. Friends and family have helped us get through these difficult times with their kindness and support in so many ways. Andy worries about me a lot and will very often ask if I'm okay. My reply would be, "It's okay, I'm on a mission," meaning that in my head I want to achieve a lot today.

As I write this, I am, along with everybody else in the country (and most of the world), in lockdown. Covid-19 has struck worldwide and has caused a pandemic the likes of which we haven't seen for years. As Andy has diabetes and a heart condition he has to work from home and I've been told that I must not work as a teaching assistant because of Andy being in the high risk category and needed shielding. Friends and colleagues are cheering each other up by texting, face timing and emailing as we are not allowed to go and see them in person. Andy and I are lucky enough to have lots of caring friends to keep us going through this tough time but, equally, we are lucky to have each other (especially him)!

Jilly Ashworth

Jilly Ashworth

Jilly Ashworth is a mum to three boys whose husband is a bilateral amputee. Jilly works two separate part-time jobs, runs the household and cares for the needs of her husband's disabilities. As well as overcoming anxiety and depression, Jilly suffers from the debilitating condition of fibromyalgia. She has a determination and a 'just get on with it' attitude that is an inspiration to all who know her.

SOCIAL MEDIA LINKS.

https://www.facebook.com/jilly.ashworth

99

Life deals you your cards,
rise to the challenge no matter
how big.
I say Bring it on!"

ANDY ASHWORTH

A Lucky Man

That feeling when you sense you're being stared at. You scan your surroundings and see a twitch of someone's head as they guiltily seek something else to focus on.

I've seen that quite a lot since it happened.

Then there are those who stare quite openly, with a look of sympathy or compassion in their eyes. I have never sought either since I've been like this. Then there are those, more confident to broach the subject, who ask, "So, what happened to you?"

I am always happy to answer since the story of how I lost my legs, and my subsequent battle to recover as best I can, is an important one to tell.

One young lady, a friend of my teenage son, asked me exactly that. I took a deep breath, primarily for dramatic effect, and asked her in return, "Have you seen the film Jaws?".

A bit cruel to her, I suppose, but those in the room who saw the look of horror on her face found it funny enough. Comedy, if you can call it that, is an important part of my ability to stay positive.

The truthful answer is that my real predator here was a set of nail clippers. As a diabetic I was told to be careful when cutting toenails. One of the many complications of diabetes is loss of circulation, particularly to feet and hands. If they get cut then there is a risk that the wound will not heal and can often take weeks or months to fix, or cause loss of toes or, worse still, loss of leg. This is what happened to me.

I rushed the job. This very simple job.

It literally nearly killed me, and I don't want anyone else to suffer the same trauma

Instead of cutting my toenail, I cut a thin slice at the tip of my second toe of my left foot which led, over several months, to me losing my left leg. Worse still, dormant infection from that episode came back two years later and through two operations over a 3-month period, I lost my right leg too. Left leg below knee (medical term – belowkneedium) and right leg above knee (abovekneedidly-dumdum). Of course, I may have made up those medical terms.

This is the first reason why telling my story is so important to me. Diabetes is a nasty disease. Most people know someone who has it, but most don't fully understand how serious it can be. It literally nearly killed me, and I don't want anyone else to suffer the same trauma my family and I have had to endure. I want people to get tested for diabetes regularly. It's simple to arrange through many local pharmacies and, if caught early, can be managed easily through diet control. I want to constantly get this message out there.

I have also discovered that by sharing my story, many people have been inspired by my attitude and determination to make the best of the cards dealt to me.

Apart from "what happened to you?" I am asked many other questions frequently. "How do you keep smiling with your situation?", "How do you keep motivated and what keeps you going?", "How do you set yourself up for each day?", "What do you want to achieve next?" and "What do you want for dinner tonight?" although that last one is less relevant to this story to be fair.

I love smiles and laughter. I've said before, I think I'm hilarious but sometimes I must admit I do sometimes have comedy "tourettes" as I often use a quick one liner to detract from my own shyness. However, there are times when people themselves appear uncomfortable seeing me with my prosthetics or if I have my stump(s) exposed but I have found a quick joke at my own expense gives them more of a sense of ease.

One example that springs to mind was when I was going into have my first operation. It was to remove two toes on my left foot. I had elected to reject a general anaesthetic and chosen a "blocker" in my knee to numb any feeling below the knee. The procedure was to go to the ante room next to theatre, where the anaesthetist explained what they would do and, for clarity, asked me to run through my understanding of who I was, date of birth and what I was having done.

Now, picture this, on my left foot, the second and third toes were both black and necrotic and a there was a big black arrow pointing down my shin and along the top of my foot indicating where they needed to attack. Regardless, I proceeded "Andy Ashworth, 13th August 1962 and I'm having two toes on my left foot amputated, but I understand that if the surgeon doesn't like what they find they may have to remove more". It seems I had passed question one and so I was wheeled through to theatre.

I was greeted by six or seven medics in green gowns at the foot of the bed. They erected a screen, so I didn't have to watch, but I once again had to run through who I was and what I was having done. Once again, I gave the right answer and so the medical team prepared to go in. Masks were in place and just as the surgeon leant forward to start, I yelled, "Woah, woah, woah." They all looked genuinely startled. So, looking directly at the surgeon with sharp implements in her hand, "When I say two toes on my left foot, it's the left from where I am looking not from where you are." Their relief was palpable, but we all got on famously throughout the rest of the procedure.

For the record I felt no pain during the operation, but I must admit hearing the snipping at my toes was slightly off putting especially when I counted more than two snips. But only two toes went that day and the consensus was all went well. Sadly, I subsequently had to have a further 4 operations over the two years since then which have resulted in my current predicament.

Generally, I love to see smiles and hear laughter, it can be infectious

Generally, I love to see smiles and hear laughter, it can be infectious and makes life seem that bit better, don't you think?

I'm reminded of a Facebook post I once had shared to me. It was posted by an Army veteran from Iraq or Afghanistan. He had lost both legs above the knee (abovekneedidlydumdi??). It went something like, "People ask me how I stay so positive after losing my legs? I simply ask them how they stay so negative with theirs." That, quite simply, could be my own motto.

I remember lying in hospital after losing my first leg. You have a lot of thinking time in hospital and rather than feeling sorry for myself I quickly decided I would explore every avenue to make the best of what I had. The coverage of the Paralympics has made us all more aware of what can be achieved by people with such challenges and so, given I was relatively young and healthy, I would try my damnedest to get back to be as mobile as I could. I worked with an amazing physio in our beloved NHS local hospital to learn techniques with a temporary leg until my stump was healed enough to be cast for my own prosthetic leg. Stubbornly it took 6 months to get to that point.

I need to have goals set as I need to satisfy a sense of achieving them. I asked what I should expect to be able to do, i.e. when should I expect to be walking without the aid of walking sticks. Six months. Well that stirred the competitor in me. Three weeks later I walked, stick free, into my physio appointment. Nailed it.

I was walking well, some people barely even noticed my slight limp, so when I fell ill at Christmas 2017 and eventually lost my right leg it was a significant step backwards, so to speak. The right leg amputation ended up above the knee, as I mentioned. This compounded the degree of difficulty I was facing. I not only have two artificial legs, but I only have one with the control of my own knee.

It's hard. Very hard.

I worked with, and nagged at, my physio and prosthetic team to accelerate getting an improved design of prosthetic as I had not taken to my original offerings.

I felt I needed to "give them something back" for giving me the chance to learn to walk again. I decided to aim to do a walk for charity. This was in March 2019, and so I set the following ambitious challenge. I would aim to walk round the boundary of my local cricket club.

Traditionally the club holds a cricket event each August Bank Holiday so I approached them to see if they would allow me to be a sideshow on the day and do my walk. They agreed and so I was committed. At this stage the furthest I had walked was just 25 metres and the boundary walk would be nearing 400 metres. There was some work to be done.

I announced the walk in April. I wanted to raise money for some special causes
    1) Diabetes UK
    2) A cancer charity (this was later to be re-focused on a
    local hospice as one of our dearest friends was lovingly

cared for but sadly lost her brave battle to cancer in July) 3) Two of the NHS teams who had helped get me to this point. The prosthetic team used the money for equipment for young amputees adjust to their new challenge and my amazing physio team who have worked with me over this three-year journey.

4) Finally, our cricket club, who have played an important part in our lives and my funds have meant that they will have an electronic scoreboard installed in time for the 2020 season.

I set up a page on a charity funding site, with the aim of raising £1000 GBP and in the July pushed out my quest to social media Facebook, Instagram and even LinkedIn. Astonishingly the total, overnight, reached £600 GBP and so I reset the target to £3000 GBP.

It's amazing how quickly time flies when you have something big to work towards!

We had a family holiday scheduled in Portugal for the two weeks leading up to the walk, so I did aim to build up some stamina with some "warm weather training". Nevertheless, by the morning of the walk I had only managed just 60 metres. It was a foolish approach, a bit like doing a marathon having only previously done 4 miles. Gulp.

The day itself was a hot one. I did question my sanity a number of times that morning but there were over 100 people there, well over 150 contributors and over £4500 GBP raised at that stage and I was not going to let anyone down.

Anyway, the walk took just under one hour to complete 360 metres. The public address systems played me home to "Simply the Best – Tina Turner". Someone had set a table at the finish line with a bottle of beer placed on it. My eldest son was in front of me at the finish, my youngest next to me and my wife was making sure my wheelchair was ready behind me. I said to my son, "Give me a hug, otherwise I might fall down." I threw my sticks away in joyful celebration and gratefully took my seat. I raised my arms in triumph and, as Tina belted out the words "simply the best", I toasted the crowd with the sweetest tasting bottle of beer I remember.

It was a very emotional moment and one I will savour for life.

In the end I raised £5200 GBP. I am still humbled by this extraordinary total.

It's important for me to have these goals, or baby steps as I call them. When the "high" of having completed the walk was over, I felt an immediate void, a real low. What next?

> It was a very emotional moment and one I will savour for life.

My story was, I am reminded frequently, an inspiration but I didn't get this. I was just getting on with making the best of the hand I'd been dealt. I was then introduced to a remarkable lady, Rebecca Adams. Rebecca is a motivational coach and mentor to people and businesses worldwide. She had heard of my personal journey and invited me to be part of her International Interview Series in 2019. I'd never done anything like that before, but Rebecca inspires you to believe you are worthy to achieve so I agreed to do it.

The process of being interviewed in itself gave me so much. It made me realise just how far I had actually come at a time when I was wondering whether I could go on any further.

Less than two years previously I had been in an induced coma for two days to recover from an operation that nearly proved fatal. Yet here I was, back on two feet (albeit artificial ones) and walking again.

The feedback from the interview from Rebecca, and others who watched it, convinced me that I could actually tell my story and make people re-evaluate their own lives and overcome their own personal struggles. It's something I'd been told but only now did I start to believe it.

I was asked to speak at the Empowerment Convention IGNITE Live Event 2021, again something I have never done or even believed I could do. I also have been asked to do some radio interviews.

Wow! Just Wow.

So, my future is not defined but new doors have been opened for me to explore.

I have my beautiful, dedicated wife who has stood by me through all this, often at personal cost to her own health. I have three sons each growing into completely different but, at the same time, fine young gentlemen. I have extraordinary support from my mum, brother and his family. I have met some amazing, inspirationally positive new friends.

Yes, I have lost my legs, but I have so much more. I am alive, and have an exciting path to tread, slowly at first and with sticks. I will plot each journey with my baby step milestones and walk there with a smile on my face and song in my heart.

I am indeed, a very lucky man. The future is bright. Bring it on.

Smashing Through the Glass Ceiling!

Andy Ashworth

Andy Ashworth

Andy is a very inspirational and amazing human being. He lost both his legs over a 3 year period through an infection complicated by diabetes. He is fighting back by learning to walk with prosthetics. Andy's recent challenge was set to walk for charity round his local cricket club boundary and he raised £5000 GBP (approx over $6400 USD) and he raised awareness of the issues diabetes can cause. Throughout his journey, Andy has been encouraged by so many people who have said to him that his story inspired them to reassess their own "challenges" in their lives and take a different view.

SOCIAL MEDIA LINKS.
https://www.facebook.com/andy.ashworth.165

99

On your journey you will get
knocked down.
You need to look up and Rise!"

JULIE DICKENS

Rise

You have been assigned this mountain to show others it can be moved.

These are the words I have said to myself repeatedly over the last eighteen months. I have been knocked down over and over again. I have experienced four out of the five most stressful life events all within a short time frame. Divorce, death of a loved one, emergency surgery, and job loss. I had two choices; to stay knocked down or rise.

I chose to RISE.

It was June 30th, 2018 and I woke up in my happy place, Aruba. Today was my seventeenth wedding anniversary. I recall the ache in my heart as I got out of bed that morning. Another year had come and gone. Another year of feeling alone, empty, unattractive, not enough. Another year of wishing things were different. Another year of pretending everything was fine. I got dressed and headed to the beach for my morning walk. Little did I know, I would be receiving a gift that morning.

I got to the beach and decided just to sit. As soon as I saw the ocean, I was flooded with emotions and began to cry. I felt like I was a failure. I had failed myself, my husband, my daughter, my parents, God. I so desperately wanted my marriage to work out, to be happy, to be in love. I knew I needed to make a decision. To be done and move on with my life, but I was scared. Would I be able to survive financially? What would this do my daughter? What would people think of me?

> ❝
> **I remember praying to God asking Him to help me. I remember asking Him to show me the way.**

I remember praying to God asking Him to help me. I remember asking Him to show me the way. And I clearly recall hearing that I am loved. I am a daughter of the King, and I have a bright future in front of me, to follow my heart.

It was in that moment, that I knew I needed to do what was best for me and that it would be okay. Four months later, I met my husband at a coffee shop and we decided it was time to end our marriage. At that time, I had a choice to make. To stay knocked down or to rise?

I chose to RISE.

Was it easy? No. But, I surrounded myself with those that lifted me up, that encouraged me and spoke life into me.

I focused on self-development and making myself the best version of me. You know the saying, "When God closes one door He opens another?" It's true! He opened a door that led to me an amazing man. I'm so happy I listened to my heart and got over my fear that day in Aruba.

While I was going through my divorce, my Mom and best friend started having health issues. She was always my biggest cheerleader, the person who I could turn to for advice, love and support. Now the tables were turned, it was my turn to be there for her.

Despite not feeling her best, my Mom always had a positive attitude, a smile on her face and was focused on others.

On August 13th, 2019 I woke up in Destin, Florida. My family and I were spending a week there vacationing before summer ended. We went parasailing that morning. It was so peaceful, I remember feeling close to God. All was right in my world.

Later that afternoon my world came crashing down around me.

I received a call from my sister that changed my life forever. My Mom was gone.

I found myself feeling like I had been punched in the stomach, like I was going to throw up. My heart felt like it had been ripped from my chest. I couldn't breathe. I remember screaming saying it couldn't be true. My head was spinning. I don't recall much after that, I guess I was in shock.

The hours, days and weeks to follow were unimaginable. How could I go on without my Mom and best friend? For the second time I had a choice to make. Would I let this keep me knocked down or would I rise?

I chose to RISE.

How did I do it? I relied heavily on my faith, which is what my Mom instilled in me. I prayed, read my bible, listened to worship music and surrounded myself with those that would lift me up. By extending grace to myself, it allowed me to know I just needed to take it a moment at a time.

It has been a year since she passed, and I try to live every day of my life to make my Mom proud. I know she speaks to me and I draw strength from the special moments we shared, conversations we had and the examples she lived out. There will always be a hole in my heart, but over time the edges are softening.

On December 16th, 2019 I had to have emergency knee surgery. I am a dance studio owner and teach dance for a living, so this was shocking news. Plus, it was eight days before Christmas! I was given the news I would not be able to travel home for the holidays to be with family. This would be the first Christmas without my mom.

Emotionally I spiraled and found myself getting depressed. Thankfully, I came through the surgery just fine, but the recovery would be a long process. It would require patience and me asking for help, both of which I am not good at. For the third time, I found myself faced with a choice. Would I stay knocked down, or would I rise?

I chose to RISE.

I got over myself and learned to ask for help. I also welcomed this opportunity to rest, it was much needed.

Recently, I resigned from a job that I had for last five and half years of my life. I was struggling with the decision but, as always, God showed up and made it clear as to what I was supposed to make. It needed to be, but, it still brought up lots of emotions for me. I was told I was not a good fit for this company and these words stung even though I know it wasn't true. I didn't want others to be disappointed in me by my decision. I felt like I had given up. And for the fourth time in a short amount of time I was faced with a choice. Would I let this keep me knocked down or would I rise?

> I know she speaks to me and I draw strength from the special moments we shared

I chose to RISE!

As I look back on the last eighteen months of my life, I have gone through a lot. These difficult situations would be enough for anyone to throw in the towel and give up. But I know I was meant for more and that is why every time I made the choice to rise.

I want you to look at me and see the mountains I have moved. And I want you to be inspired to find your strength to move your own mountains in your life!

In Dedication

I dedicate this to my Mom, my best friend and angel. Thank you for being the best Mom to me, I was truly blessed God chose you as my Mom. You have taught me so many valuable lessons throughout my life. I will continue to draw from them as I continue forward on my journey. I miss and love you so much. Even though you are not here I know you are beside me loving me always and forever.

To Marley, my daughter and reason for being. I know we have been through a lot in the last eighteen months. I always want you to remember there will be dark moments in life. Never, ever give up. Rely on your faith in the Lord, the love of your family and friends. And always, no matter what, choose to Rise.

To my love, Brian Prosser. Thank you for showing me what love is again. You have supported me through the darkest moments of my life. You've held me up when I couldn't stand and encouraged me along the way. Thank you for being my best friend, my love and my partner in life. God heard my prayers and answered them by placing you into my life at the exact moment I needed you most. I love you!

Julie Dickens

Julie Dickens

Julie Dickens is the Director and CEO of JDM School of Dance, based in McKinney, Texas. She is also the owner of Doodycalls Pet Waste Removal Service. She has been in business for many years and is an advocate for health and wellness.

Julie has been featured in magazines, on TV Channels in the USA and her brand and business is expanding exponentially.

She is a proud Mom and is a dedicated Partner.
She is also a Dog Mama too.

WEB LINKS.

Facebook - https://www.facebook.com/julie.roachdickens
Website - https://jdmschoolofdance.com/
JDM Facebook - https://www.facebook.com/JdmSchoolOfDance
JDM Instagram – https://www.instagram.com/jdmschoolofdance
Doodycalls Facebook - https://www.facebook.com/Doody-Calls-Pet-Waste-Removal-Service-of-Dallas-Texas-102987447332

"

Facing your demons
is no easy road to travel on,
it takes work and courage"

LISA LOWNDES

Living in Fear

As a small child, I was always shy, quiet and never one to ask for anything. I grew up in London with my Mum and younger sister.

My Nan and dear Grandad lived in Essex.

Much of my childhood school summer holidays were spent at Southend Seafront and I'll always remember my sister and I quietly playing with the sand and my Mum commenting that we were 'odd children that never even asked for an ice cream'.

In reality, much of my time was spent living in fear.

You see, I loved visiting the beach and being with my Grandad was an escape. He was my everything. My hero and the person I looked up to and admired the most. He was the only person to show me love and kindness and despite him passing away some 28 years ago, he will forever remain in my heart.

My sister was born in 1986 and I was so excited to be getting a new baby! That excitement was tinged with sadness and fear as I knew what my sister was coming into, a world of drugs, alcohol and violence. At the young age of 6 I'd spent many times hiding in my room or trying to protect my Mum. I can remember, as clear as day, the afternoon I thought my Mum and unborn baby sister would die.

I can never recall any fear for my life, but I knew I'd do anything to protect my Mum, and this particular afternoon we had been sitting in my bedroom and I went to get something from another room. It was then that I witnessed my sister's biological dad put a knife in his shoe.

My sister's father was an alcoholic and our flat was often filled with their friends who were either on drugs or drunk. It was all I knew. My own father left when I was a baby and I had very little contact with him.

I was used to seeing violence. From what I can recall, it was the norm for couples to physically fight.

Looking back, I probably assumed that's how every family lived, and growing up in Tottenham, I was used to seeing violence. From what I can recall, it was the norm for couples to physically fight.

Shortly after the arrival of my sister, her dad left. I'm unsure of the circumstances surrounding him leaving but we were also transferred to a new flat. We moved from our top floor flat to a ground floor flat in the block opposite, within the same estate. I guess I thought life might change to some degree, but little did I know the hell that was about to unfold, although equally it was also the catalyst for my entire life changing for the better.

Before I knew it my Mum had a new partner. He seemed nice, very charming and my mum seemed happy. It wouldn't be long however before that mask slipped. As some of us know, the charade won't last because once they've got you hooked and under their control, the true colours start to appear.

Once again, our home was filled with drug-induced friends and often lots of laughter. But behind that laughter the arguing had started and, again, I had to watch my Mum being physically and mentally abused. My sister's father was an alcoholic and although it never excused his behaviour, I could always make sense of it. This new man however was pure evil, like he was born a monster purely to terrify women.

Dinner time became a time of dread. I had to say what the time was when dinner was put on the table but in reality, I wasn't old enough to tell the time. I soon learned though because if I got it wrong the words that were thrown at me were too hurtful. I permanently shook through fear and I was constantly in and out of hospital as I was asthmatic. I was having asthma attacks several times a week with no apparent trigger. Looking back, I now wonder if my attacks were triggered by constant fear.

My primary school was close to a small shopping centre and my Mum and I would often pop in on our way home. There was a lovely sweet shop in the centre and Mum would buy bags of rhubarb and custard sweets 'because it would keep him in a good mood'. It worked sometimes, or at least for a few hours, but that good mood would never last. It wasn't until I was older that I became aware of the signs and behaviours of domestic abuse.

One night I was laying in bed and I could hear a commotion coming from the bathroom. I could hear the taps running, 'the devil' was shouting and I could hear our dog yelping. I crept up to the door, our bathroom was almost opposite my bedroom, and I could see that our dog was in the bath, being pushed under the water. Our poor, defenceless dog was being stabbed in the head. The sounds and images are something I can never erase from my mind and it wasn't until recently I was able to share this layer of my life to a friend. It seemed that this man was capable of anything and I wondered whether I would ever have to watch my Mum being stabbed, for the second time in my young life.

My best friend Lisa was my escape. I often spent my time at her flat and would sleep over at weekends, but her dad was an alcoholic and instead of being asleep, I would often hear him shouting at her Mum. I would always wonder whether her Mum suffered the same way, but I guess I also didn't know any different so maybe this was how families lived their lives. Maybe this is what happens when you grow up and meet a man.

My sister and I continued to spend school holidays with my Nan and Grandad in Essex. I wasn't close to my Nan, but I loved the time I got to have with my Grandad. We would go on long dog walks in their local nature reserve, it was a chance to smile and not be fearful of what would come next. He taught me about the tree's and nature and how to use a compass. We would spend ages together reading the newspaper and smiling. He loved photography and cooking; my favourite was when he made lemon curd. It was weeks of being carefree, of being the child I was supposed to be.

On one occasion when my Mum came to collect us, I refused to go home. I did everything to delay the inevitable and it's another image and sound I'll never forget. I was gripping the door handle screaming and begging my Grandad to let me stay. I was wearing wellie boots and my Mum had hold of my legs trying to pull me free from the handle. It was later in my life that I discovered both my sister and I were on the social services at risk register and my Grandparents had tried to apply for custody.

My bed in my room was a cabin bed with a desk space underneath. I loved my bed and created a little office underneath where I pretended to be a post office. I was obsessed with running a shop and I'm sure its where my stationary addiction stems from!

One day our home was raided by the police. I was told it was a 'drug bust' and our flat was ripped apart. Some of the police officers came into my bedroom and wanted to talk to me about the numbers that I'd written down on my pieces of paper. I remember at the time thinking 'I'm just pretending to be a post office lady silly Police', what would I know about drugs or dealing! The next day I went to school and told my friends, like it was the most normal thing in the world to happen.

The day my future was about to change meant the day another woman's life would never be the same again.

My Mum was crying. The 'devil' was packing his things and leaving. Inside I was smiling but I needed to comfort my Mum, hold her tight. She told me he was moving in with a lady he'd been seeing, and I couldn't believe my luck. What I also realised however was that this meant another human would suffer at his hands and I've often felt guilty for being happy to be rid of him from our lives. Sadly, we were later told that this lady lost her child to social services and I can only imagine that she suffered even worse than my Mum, because I always think - why were we never removed?

> **The day my future was about to change meant the day another woman's life would never be the same again.**

It was shortly after this happened that I was told I wouldn't be going back to school. My Mum literally packed our car out with our belongings and announced we were moving to Cambridge. We didn't have anywhere to go so we sat for hours at one of the council offices, waiting to know where we'd be spending the night.

We were placed in a temporary hostel for the time-being and a few weeks later we moved into a bungalow that was shared with another family. It was about a year later that we were given a permanent home. In the meantime, I was doing well at school and making new friends.

To some degree life was 'normal'. There was no longer the violence, but my Mum continued to spiral into a dark depression and it wasn't long before I realised she was bulimic. As a young teenager my sister suffered with anorexia and I quickly developed similar habits when dealing with difficult situations.

The biggest blow of my life came one Friday when I'd returned from a school trip. I could sense from my Mum that something was wrong but what I wasn't expecting was the news that my beloved Grandad had passed away. He had in fact died the weekend before, but mum said she didn't know how to break the news and she didn't want to ruin my school trip.

After everything that had happened, this felt like the biggest soul-destroying crush of all and a piece of me died that day too. I didn't know how I was going to carry on. I didn't know whether I'd ever feel the same way again and it reinforced that anything good in life would be snatched away. I was so devastated that it would be ten years before I could even say his name without becoming hysterical.

> ## It reinforced that anything good in life would be snatched away

When I became a parent for the first time it gave me a sense of understanding about the world. I realised even more that children shouldn't witness horror and hatred. Children should be filled with laughter, memories, self-worth and confidence. It was also when I became a Mum that I suddenly gained a sense of peace and knew it was time to let go of my grief. In my mind it was time to lay my Grandad to rest because I knew that no matter what, he would always be with me and if there was one thing I knew for certain - he would want me to be happy again. It was like a sudden bolt of clarity. It was time to let go of everything, try to forgive and move on.

I spent many years continuing to feel worthless, my self-esteem was non-existent, and I believe that's what led me into toxic relationships. Something I vowed I'd never do! But it happens.

I spent many years in counselling and having Cognitive Behavioural Therapy and what I did start to realise, slowly but surely, is that not everyone is out to hurt you. That there are kind, loving people in the world. I still didn't believe I'd ever live happily ever after. In my mind that just happens in story books, but it was a start.

Becoming a Mum for the second time I realised I needed to break the old cycles. How could I raise my children to believe in themselves and their abilities if I had no belief in myself?

It was also my mission to show my Grandad that I'd made something of myself, that he could rest knowing I'd be okay and no longer suffering.

Facing your demons is no easy road to travel on, it takes work and courage and it was only last year (2019) that I had a massive turning point. That pivotal moment came when I cried because a close friend told me how grateful she was to have me in her life. I cried because I couldn't understand why she would be grateful. What did I bring? What use was I to anyone? It was like a bolt of lightning hit me there and then, something had to change and change fast.

Again, I asked myself the question of how could I preach to others about self-worth and raise my children to love themselves for who they are when I'm being a hypocrite?!

I started working on myself every day, tackling my limiting beliefs because in no way would I be a victim of my past. I was not defined by my childhood. Instead I was a warrior, a survivor and a damn good parent.

All the anger and resentment that had consumed me, I chipped away at to release it. I didn't want the burden of other people's actions on my shoulders and the sense of relief and freedom was amazing. I started to turn that shy girl who shook, into a powerful, knows what she wants woman with a voice.

I want every person who has suffered, or still suffering to know that anything is possible and you can absolutely find light at the end of the tunnel.

If you want to change, make that change.

It's scary, it can be overwhelming, it brings up triggers. But I'm simply not prepared to allow my children to require therapy because of my own actions. I wouldn't change anything that has happened to me, I see it all as lessons, that it's shaped me into who I am today and that person I am today, I am so proud of.

Dedication

I want to dedicate this chapter to my late Grandad. A day doesn't go by that I don't think of you, imagining you coming around to see your grandchildren but I know you're always watching and you're smiling with me saying 'that's my girl'. I did it Grandad! I broke the cycles, I survived, I have a loving family and I'm happy.

I also want to dedicate this chapter to my Mum. Look at everything you've ever been through and everything you've survived. You did it too! I'm very proud of you, I forgave you a long time ago and there is no need or time for any more guilt.
I love you dearly.

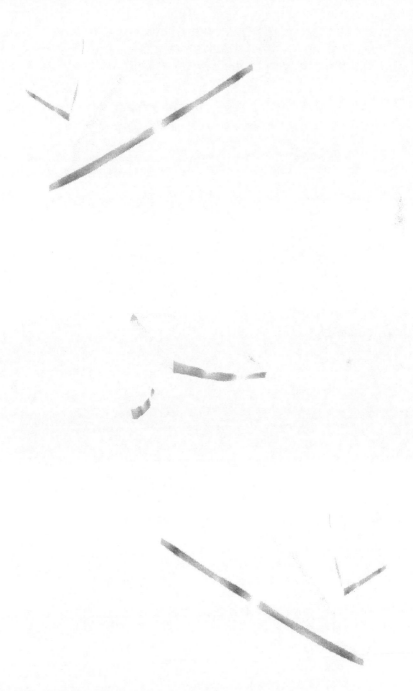

Lisa Lowndes

Lisa Lowndes

Lisa Lowndes is a mum to three boys who used to live a life of sadness & regret.

She is proof that mindset works and after letting go of the past, she now lives a happy & fulfilled life in Cambridgeshire, UK.

Lisa is health & wellbeing advocate who has overcome depression, post-natal depression, abuse and a poor relationship with food.

She designs and creates "Eat The Rainbow" Reward Charts and products to help encourage children to eat a more healthy, colourful and fulfilled diet to help nourish their bodies from the inside out.

WEB LINKS.

Personal Facebook page: https://www.facebook.com/lisa.munro.73
Facebook group: https://www.facebook.com/groups/43220976735948
8/?ref=share
Instagram: www.instagram.com/busy_with_her_kingdom
Website: https://www.lisalowndes.biz

"

Don't let the struggles of bad experiences hold you back from enjoying and living life"

TIMOTHY PARENT

Fear to Freedom

Childhood should be a time of enjoyment, fun, learning and adventure don't you think?

A time when you discover what you enjoy and over time you discover what you want to do later in life.

It should not be a time of fear, of being scared and trying to figure out where you fit in with your own family.

We were a family of five. There was Mom, Dad, my older sister aka "Daddy's little princess", my younger brother aka "Mommy's special boy". Each one of my siblings, respectively, could do no wrong in my parent's eyes. Then there was me {middle child} Nobody's "little anything". The true black sheep of the family, but not by choice.

My time was mostly spent listening very carefully to mom and dad's directions to make sure I did everything as instructed or face dire consequences. I learned early on the feeling of my dad's leather belt on my bare backside and my mom's crisp slaps across the face if things were not carried out exactly as directed.

If they had to ask questions about why things were done the way they were, I was apparently "talking back to them" when I answered their questions and I faced the taste of my dad's grease fighting bar of soap as he cut pieces from it for me to eat for the transgressions of answering those questions.

Even if I carried out tasks as asked or directed and received the rare 'Thank you', I was always afraid of when the "other shoe" would drop so to say.

One particularly rare evening after dinner, my parents decided they would go grocery shopping and during the time that they were gone we had permission to watch TV (a very rare occurrence). Since we had a family farm and my parents were also building their dream home, so according to my dad, there was no time to waste by watching tv. The only caveat to this is we were each given a chore to complete and they all had to be completed before the TV could be turned on and we could only watch what my parents allowed us to.

I was very excited because my chore was easy on this evening and I was being included in a rare "fun" activity with my siblings. Immediately upon finishing dinner and taking my dishes to the sink for my sister to wash, I set about completing my chore, which was for the trash to be taken out and a new liner being placed in the trashcan. This was a challenging chore as at that time, I was barely larger than the trash can.

> **Even if I carried out tasks as asked or directed and received the rare 'Thank you', I was always afraid**

I removed the full trash bag from the can and immediately put in the new liner and began the actual chore of taking the trash bag, that was bigger than me at the time, outside to the garbage. Upon completing my chore, I found a comfortable place on the sofa and patiently waited for my siblings to complete their tasks as I was very happy for this evening.

When my parents returned with the groceries, the television was immediately turned off and all three of us helped carry the groceries brought into the house where my parents were putting the purchased goods in the cupboards. When we finished bringing the groceries in, our parents said we could finish watching the tv program until it was over.

As I was sitting on the sofa, my mom called out to me and thanked me for completing my chore, I of course responded with a happy "You're Welcome". She did this 2-3 more times and I did not understand why she was thanking me repeatedly. I always replied in the same manner.

A few moments after the last time she thanked me, as I was sitting there quietly watching tv and enjoying it, all of a sudden, I felt the worst pain possible on the top of my head that I have, to date, experienced.

Then, I noticed beside me was a 5 pound can of tomatoes or some vegetables. So, I picked it up and gave it back to my mom thinking it must have been pushed off the counter by mistake and landed on my head. Much to my horror, my mom explained she had purposely dropped it on my head to get my attention.

When I asked why she had done this and how bad it hurt, she again thanked me for completing my chore, to which I said "You're welcome" again. I was confused because the look on my face as I looked towards my dad must have said it all, because he did something he rarely, if ever did for me. He actually stood up for me and took my side and told my mom that each time she thanked me I said "you're welcome" so I was not ignoring her. She said to my dad "You are missing the point. He did not do as he was told. He did not complete his chore!".

For a moment fear raced through me like it never had before and I thought, "Did I imagine completing my chore or did my siblings pull a mean prank on me and bring the trash back into the house?"

I immediately began mentally preparing myself for the continued punishment that I could only imagine was coming if when my dad opened the trash can and found it full of trash. Much to my relief and pure joy, when he opened it, it was empty with a new liner. I was so overjoyed I almost called out with pure delight.

Dad showed my mom that I had completed the chore I was given and asked her why she thought it wasn't complete if she had not even checked. To my sadness she replied, "well, look at who we are talking about, the complete screwup, do I need to say more?"

So, I was punished and ridiculed for doing what I was asked. And the worst part was having a clearer understanding of how my mom felt about me, her oldest son.
I never gave up trying to please my parents and do exactly as directed. I knew someday the opportunity would present itself for me to be on my own and away from what I considered a hellish childhood spent either alone, doing chores for my parents or being punished even when there was no reason.

It was one of those hot summer days where it felt like the heat would never end and there was no relief from it. Even though I was only 12 years old, it was one of those days that stays in my mind like it happened yesterday.

This day I was excited because lunchtime was coming soon and we would not only catch a break from working on the family farm & escape the heat for a while, but my mom was also making what I thought was one of the best meals I had ever tasted - homemade tacos and I loved them, so I was super excited for lunch that day since at that time I could easily eat a dozen or more of what I considered to be the world's best tacos!

As I sat at the dining room table with my family it was obvious that I was in a very good mood and very happy. We talked as a family and as we were joking around, I came down with a case of the giggles. No matter what anybody said I could not stop laughing and for some reason this very much irritated my mother, which became very obvious as she began hollering at me to stop laughing. No matter how much I tried, the more I laughed and giggled, my mom got even more irritated and angry.

After what seemed to be a short while, my mom got up from the table and walked over to me and got right in my face hollering at me and telling me to stop laughing or she was going to punish me. What didn't surprise me was that she was not upset at my siblings, who were also giggling and laughing. In thinking about it, they were probably laughing because I was, after all laughing is contagious like yawning is. But, as my mom was in my face and hollering at me and threatening punishment, it only caused me to laugh that much harder.

At that point my mom became very angry and began slapping me all across my face and head in order to get me to stop. I was confused because I was happy and laughing and it made her mad to the point of hitting me and when her hitting me did not work in reducing or stopping me from laughing, she picked me up by my shoulders and pushed me up against the wall which was right next to the table.

And of course, that did not work as I continued laughing so she then grabbed me by my ears and began pulling my head towards her and then slamming my head against the wall. My mom was hitting my head against the wall so hard that the wall actually cracked. This made her even more angry, so she began hitting my head against the wall even harder and at that point my head split open and I began to bleed.

> **I was confused because I was happy and laughing and it made her mad to the point**

And because of the pain this caused me, I did stop laughing and began crying, which seemed to bring my mother joy, but she did not stop. She continued to a point that I was ready to pass out from the pain. During this whole incident she was hollering insults at me and when she finally did stop, she said that I deserved everything that I got, and this will teach me a lesson to not act like that at the dinner table and to do as she says.

I was very confused by her comment as I sat there bleeding and holding a napkin on my head to catch the bleeding. Why was it inappropriate to be in a good mood to the point you come down with the giggles and laughter? And why was it only inappropriate for me and not my siblings?

We didn't have company. It was our family, and why is it such a bad thing to be in a great mood and be excited about a great meal?

My brother and sister were laughing just as hard as I was, and my dad was smiling at us. Why was my mom so angered and only with me?

> "
> # This was my first lesson on the need to be more precise about what I wanted.

I did not eat much that meal after all and I remembered thinking, as I had on many other occasions such as this, that one day hopefully in the near future, I will have the opportunity to leave, hopefully to be on my own but mostly to be away from these sorts of treatments. This was my first lesson on the need to be more precise about what I wanted.

I did get part of my desire by having an opportunity to leave home. Unfortunately, I was placed in a much worse situation simply because I was unaware that my thoughts not only went into the universe about my desires, but also that you need to be aware of what you're wishing for because you just may get it. But that is for another time.

I did, through a conversation with my maternal grandmother discover why my mom seemed to take out a lot of anger on me and why it seemed she was always angry with me, even if I did what she asked.

Apparently, I reminded her of my birth father beginning at a very young age and in multiple ways. From the way I talked, walked, carried myself and my laugh. And when she witnessed any of this, it triggered her anger towards my birth father and she took it out on me.

I would never wish any of my childhood experiences at home on anybody. However, all of those experiences made me stronger so I could handle the next chapter in my life.

No matter what has happened to you in the past don't let it hold you back, don't feel diminished, don't let people talk down to you, don't let people make you feel like you're less than you are because you're wonderful.

What happened to you in your past, especially when you were a child, was not your fault, it was beyond your control. And look at you now. You are a stronger person because you made it through that experience and you can handle anything that is in your path now and might be in the future, and you will make it!

As my mentor always says to me you are worthy, you are strong enough, you will make it and keep going always, it's worth it and you're worth it.

Timothy Parent

Timothy Parent

Timothy Parent inspires to bring about empowered, positive change for people everywhere. He is a New York Times best-selling co-author in 2 categories, a certified Law of Attraction Practitioner and a life coach in training.

Timothy is also known by some as "The Miracle Walking Man".

He loves tacos, trucks and dogs. He lives in Arizona, USA.

WEB LINKS:

Facebook: https://www.facebook.com/timothy.parent/

99

Let the beauty of the everyday sustain you"

SHERRY CANNON-JONES

Re-awaking of the Soul

As a Soul's Purpose Strategist, my work gives me the perfect opportunity to live a life that lights up my soul, connects me to my purpose, gifting me a continual sense of joy to see beauty, have a grateful heart, happiness and fulfilment in the everyday. It's about living my best life now and being the best version of me I can be in our Garden of Life.

I have always felt a calling to be able to make a difference in the lives of others and for 21 years it was as a teacher. Now I get to transfer that passion to make a difference in the lives of people all over the world. To transform someone's life from one of over-whelm and apathy to one of joy, peace and abundance feeds my soul.

Life has not always been this way.

I have been on a tremendous journey of self-discovery and re-connected with my authentic self. I am sharing with you some of the challenges I have faced and overcome in my lifetime to find myself in the present moment - which is one filled with peace, hopefulness, passion, gratitude and motivation. I now have the best mission in the world, it lights a fire in my belly, but life wasn't always like this for me...

Three years ago, I was stressed and in the midst of anxiety and de-pression following the death of my mum. I woke up each day with a numbness that was only ever replaced by a sense of overwhelm if I tried to break free from it. My relationships were crumbling, and I had no self-worth or sense of identity, there was no passion for life and there was a distinct lack of fun and laughter. For years I had allowed others to take control and steer the direction of my life. Gradually, my identity and confidence had all but vanished. Outwardly, I still wore the mask of the strong, confident and resil-ient girl I had been as a child but inside I was lost.

> **Somewhere deep inside was a voice, a spirit that wasn't going to give up.**

I didn't know who I was or what my path or purpose was in life. The loss of my mum had completely rocked my foundations, leaving me lost in the rubble of my life.

Somewhere deep inside was a voice, a spirit that wasn't going to give up. As I listened to it, I knew there was defi-nitely more living to do. My soul was reminding me I had a purpose and I just needed to reconnect with it. The more help and support I sought out, the stronger my inner voice grew en-couraging me on.

I started to take care of me ... I nour-ished my mind, body and spirit so I could get back to being the best ver-sion of me there was.

With this came a clarity of truth, I could see the warning markers that had been there over the years that I had ignored, the contin-ual drawing on reserves of strength and resilience but never top-ping them back up... the handing over control to others leading me on a path I wasn't meant to be on.

Once I reconnected with my truth, the path to reigniting my soul's purpose was clear. I was able to free myself from the limiting beliefs, expectations and pressures I had allowed life and other people to place on me but let's start at the beginning:

Born in 1969 weighing just 5lbs, I came into the world in just the same way as my life was to unfold, on a mission. Although I initially gained strength and weight well, and appeared to be thriving, I soon developed complications with my lungs, and I began a battle to stay alive.

I became a long-term patient at London's Great Ormond Street Hospital and my fight to live began for sure. To my knowledge I was given end of life prayers by the duty Chaplain on at least 3 occasions. Each time I fell ill, my parents were told I wouldn't live until my next birthday and each time I reached that birthday, doctors gave them another deadline. Fulltime hospital was my home until just before my 3rd birthday, but I continued over the year to be in and out of hospital until finally after my last hospitalisation, aged 10, the doctors said anything from that point was 'borrowed time'.

Well at aged 51 I am incredibly grateful that God has allowed me to stay and continues to have great plans for me. I grew up in a loving family, I was a happy, sociable and conscientious child, apart from the usual teenage angst that most of us go through I had a pretty steady adolescence. I married my childhood sweetheart at 19 and we were married for 13 years and have two gorgeous boys. At the age of 32 the marriage broke down and I found myself adrift for the first time in my adult life after spending over half my life with this one person.

Over time, I had alienated myself from my family, as the relationship between them and my husband wasn't great. Through their eyes they had seen a happy, confident, self-assured girl lose herself to a self-critical, unavailable and often very sad replacement. The spark had gone. There was very little passion and zest for life left in my eyes.

I had achieved some great things in that time, giving birth and raising two beautiful boys. My wish, as a child, was to get married and raise a large family. I loved the idea of running a home that was filled with love and happiness. When I married in 1988 that is exactly how I thought it would pan out. In reality, it was not to be the case.

Self-doubt and a lack of self-respect grew over the years and saw me accept things that in my younger years I would have never allowed to happen. An attempt to address this, came in the form of me going to university and becoming a teacher and as my marriage ended, I secured a job I loved and moved into my own house in my hometown. But I had in fact lost 'me'.

Being on my own with two small boys was a pivot point. I began to claim my life back. I rebuilt the closeness to my parents whom I saw all the time instead of occasionally and I reconnected with friends. Now I was beginning to regain a sense of self. I remember how good it felt to know I was able to start thinking for myself again and make my own decisions.

To embrace my new sense of independence, I decided to completely gut and redesign my bedroom to make it a place of beauty, peace and restoration at the end of a hard day raising two boisterous boys under 3 and working part time as a teacher. It was during this process I met a lady who has become one of my lifelong friends.

Across the road was an empty skip in a neighbour's garden, a casual hello found me asking if I might add my things and the rest, as they say, is history. Another chance meeting with her neighbour struck up the second friendship and we had ourselves a group of single girls who cemented friendships that would feed and support us for the next few years before we all moved.

The 'Charlton Road Girls', as we called ourselves, was definitely a lesson in how powerful positive relationships can be, surrounding yourself with people who support and uplift you, makes you view the world very differently. Their friendships are a source of strength and positivity that remains to this day and although we see each other far less these days they will be friendships that remain with me forever.

Life began to feel good again and I was rediscovering who I was. Thoughts and attitudes from when I was a girl, would remind me of the kind of person I used to be and the things that made me happy and what I felt were important and made a difference. My faith, was again, an important part of my life and I started to attend church regularly.

I knew that part of living a good life was to help others and when 9/11 occurred, the church were sending a volunteer party out to help with the soup kitchens. At this point I was faced with all the negativity again about what value to the world I had to offer. The boy's dad was unwilling to look after them in order to allow me to go to America for 2 weeks and asked what I thought 'Sherry Paget' (as I was then) could do that would be of any help to the people at ground zero.

> "
> **I was faced with all the negativity again about what value to the world I had to offer.**

I was crushed all over again, who did I think I was? why would I think I had anything to offer anybody? I hadn't been enough to keep a husband from wandering throughout my marriage and now I was on my own.

Thankfully, the love I received from family and friends gradually restored my belief in me and after changing jobs to a local school, I set about finishing the renovations of the house and making a loving home for myself and the boys.

Life felt good again.

We were making memories and it was good. I soon found that respite every fortnight became time for me to relax and chill and rejuvenate. I spent time with the 'Charlton Road Girls' and I was truly on a journey of self-discovery. My parents visited often and on one such occasion I remember walking in on my mum crying.

When I asked her what was wrong, she said she had heard me laughing in the other room and it was the first time in years she had heard that pure joyous belly laugh from me and she realised her 'daughter' was back.

Over the next 10 years I got married again and moved to France. For many reasons this was a decision I would not take again but I made some life-long friendships and will be eternally grateful for those. Although the marriage failed, we're still very good friends and I have been able to see that the ending of a relationship does not always have to result in conflict and aggression, which leaves you stripped emotionally and with no self-confident. I was able to move on with a positive outlook and take the good emotions and thoughts with me.

> **I lost sight of what was important and, in an attempt to please everyone**

I did realise that I had the habit of allowing people to control my thoughts and actions. I never really strived to be in charge of my own destiny. I lost sight of what was important and, in an attempt to please everyone, I pleased no-one. I had allowed my faith to weaken and stopped living a life that centred around the teachings of Jesus. I believe that has an impact on the thoughts we have and the actions we carry out and I lost sight of me for the second time.

Emotionally I was at a low point and made decisions that, at the time, I thought were the correct ones for people concerned rather than myself. The outcome was I set my life on a path that has since that day felt like second best. It has often been all consuming. It comes from the realisation I cannot change the past. When I allow myself to face that realisation head on, it can literally feel like my heart is breaking. It's only recently that I can see it is something I need to deal with. I am beginning to face the fear of how it feels to deal with the feelings and finally learn to forgive myself and let the guilt go. Without that process, it is impossible to truly move on and fulfil the potential in life you were destined for.

Despite not having a great sense of love for myself, life decided that love was to find me again and in October 2015 Scott proposed to me while we were on a trip to Las Vegas. I now share my life with someone who surrounds me with love, support and extends that to all those around me. He showed me what it was like to share your life with someone who wants the best for you and knows you better than you know yourself at times. There is no control. Actions and words come from a place of mutual love and respect and a common goal to build a life together equally.

When those around you love and support you, the best version of you emerges, and in the times when you are not at your best, their unconditional love carries you through any feelings of doubt or guilt. That person doesn't have to be a partner, they can be a parent, sibling, dependant or friend, just someone you know that loves you unconditionally.

I view my life so far as an incredible journey, and I look back at how far I have come. After a couple of really challenging years, starting with being frighteningly close to losing my life again after 38 years, I made the decision that things had to change. My life has had its share of ups and downs, starting from fighting for my life as a baby to falling into the depths of depression after losing my mum in Oct 2016.

Losing her has to be the hardest thing in my life that I have been faced with. Being 48 I really wasn't prepared for the feeling of being 'lost' that engulfed me. I may as well have been 10 years old.

As I was growing up I always dreaded the thought of losing a parent but in recent years I began to accept it was part of life and although I knew it would be painful, I thought it would be a grieving process that I would go through just like anyone else and life would just carry on.

Wow, how wrong was I? I was totally unprepared, although I spent the last week of her life by her bedside awaiting the inevitable, I actually never really accepted it was going to happen and when it did, I felt like I had died too.

People kept saying it would get better and life would get back to 'normal' after the funeral. I was expected back to work the day after the funeral. I look back now and I think my mind was shutting down.

On the day of the funeral I remember an overwhelming sense of complete numbness after I had done my reading. When I returned to the pew, the physical pain was unbearable, I felt like my chest was being crushed and for a few moments I truly thought I was dying and would be joining my mum.

From that point on I sank deeper and deeper into a dark place, the doctor signed me off from work and I literally gave up. Life had no meaning, although I still had the people I loved around me, I felt like a lost little girl. I cancelled my up-coming hen weekend and, along with my dad, we pretty much didn't leave the house. I spent the majority of my days crying and could speak to no-one as the words wouldn't come out.

Our forthcoming wedding was the only thing I could use to drag myself through each day. There had been thoughts of cancelling but as a family we needed something positive to focus on and my mum would not have wanted me to change it.

The day itself was beautiful and it gave everyone some much needed positivity. Mentally and emotionally I was not in the best place and the day actually felt very surreal for me, much like what I imagine an out of body experience would feel like. We went off on honeymoon and my dad went to stay with my brother for Christmas and New Year. Being away helped in many ways and the peace and tranquillity of Bali fed my spirit in a way that is hard to describe. There is a sense of healing all round and as a non-Christian country, Christmas is not celebrated which suited me just fine. Scott and I shared quiet, intimate days and I was relieved not to have to face the expectation of having fun and enjoyment for the first Christmas without mum.

The next morning, which was Christmas Day, we received a call from my brother to say my Dad had had a heart attack and was in hospital.

Again, the world came crashing down, I was halfway around the world and in danger of losing my second parent in the space of months. We spend the next two days in limbo. After many reassurances he was going to be fine, we stayed for the remainder of our honeymoon and tried to make the best of it. When we got home, I knew taking care of my Dad was now my main priority.

I believe it is my grit, determination and that 'fighting spirit', coupled with a genuine need to care and serve others that has enabled me to come through these life challenges. I believe your past is what brings you to the person you are in the present. I left the teaching profession to become my Dad's full-time carer. It was at this time I decided things had to change and I needed to find a path that would reignite my dreams which had been lost along the way.

> "
> I believe it is my grit, determination and that 'fighting spirit', coupled with a genuine need to care and serve others

Now I live a life that is grounded in simple abundance, loving relationships, a growing business making a difference to others. It's the joy of the everyday that sustains me when the challenges of life come knocking. I rediscovered my sense of self and my authentic essence as I reawakened my spiritual faith. You have everything you need inside yourself to unlock a life of joy, peace and fulfilment. Sometimes you just need a helping hand to connect with it. And this is why I do what I do ...

I help women rebuild their broken or lost spirit through reconnecting them with their sense of self and inner voice. Guiding to re-awaken your soul and reignite your passion for life, identifying the things that bring joy, in accordance with how God created your life to be. To connect with your soul's purpose to free you to live a life of abundance through options, choice and opportunities.

Sherry Cannon-Jones

Sherry Cannon-Jones

Sherry Cannon-Jones is the Soul Purpose Strategist who helps people to reconnect with their soul's purpose and reignite their passion for life.

She was a teacher for over 20 years and she has also been in retail and customer services. She works with people who have special needs and is an entrepreneur, coach and mentor.
Sherry is based in Somerset, UK and is a Mum, Wife and daughter. She is a Special Needs Advocate and her dream or focus as a child was to "make a difference of the lives of others".

WEB LINKS:

Website: www.sherrycannonjones.com
Facebook: https://www.facebook.com/Thesoulspurposestrategist
Facebook: https://www.facebook.com/TheInspiritedFighterBusiness
Instagram: https://www.instagram.com/sherrycannonjonescoaching

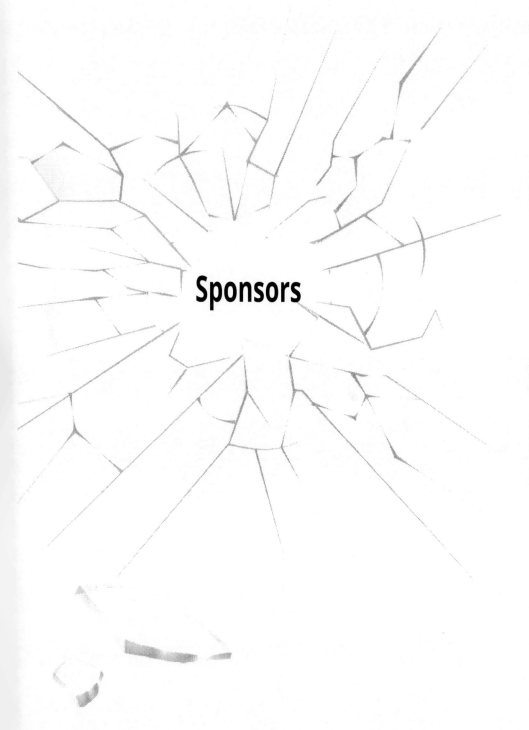

Sponsors

FEEL ALIVE AND LIVE A PHENOMENAL LIFE

Rebecca offers a huge range of opportunities to work with her to empower yourself with all areas of your life and business through her online digital programs, private bespoke coaching and much more.

Rebecca loves to share her highly positive energy with as many people around the world and if you stay with her long enough, she'll inspire and motivate you and empower your mindset so you know that you can achieve anything.

Available at all different price points you can tap into Rebecca's work at whatever level you are at too.
Connect with her on her website below.

Rebecca Adams

www.rebeccaadamsbiz.com

In inspiring people to find their own unique voice,by connecting through creativity, Ray Coates has designed a variety of services, products and programs. One of these incredible offerings is 'Songwriting - Writing YOUR Unique DNA Songs', that takes you inside and gives you accelerated insight, into Rays 40 years of songwriting, lyrical and poetic experience. Experience that has included writing a song for a major cancer docu-series aired on the WGN network in the USA from April 2020 *(Ray was also credited as a music supervisor for the series).*

Rays Songwriting coaching program enables you to write your poetry, write your lyrical thoughts and get the song out of you, that is within you. Invest in your birthright creativity. Find the keys to unlocking, inviting and welcoming even more inspirational creativity. It's time for you to write YOUR song. Creativity is to be shared and Ray shares tips, secrets and a wealth of creative intuition with you.Step inside, find and write your own, or a loved ones signature song.'Songwriting - Writing YOUR Own Unique DNA Songs'.

Visit **www.raycoatesvoice.com/products** to order and gain your lifetime access to this unique creativity program.

JENNY FORD
"Prisoner Within"
Nominated for a Prestigious Global Award 2018

Trapped in a world of nightmares and adversity, **"Prisoner Within"** tells the story of an ordinary woman on her journey desperately looking for inner peace. This fiction story has something special about it - a message that will bring much healing as a lot of people will resonate with Amy, the main character in the book.

It is a powerful and moving book about FORGIVENESS. It shows how we can be chained to past events, but once we forgive and let go, we can then unlock that prison within our mind and may be free to live a happier life. Our situations may be different but our stories will be the same.

Visit **www.jennyfordauthor.com** to purchase your book and follow Amy on her emotional and life-changing journey.

'Eat The Rainbow' Reward Charts ©

Lisa Lowndes is a Health & Wellbeing Advocate

who has overcome depression, post-natal depression, abuse and a poor relationship with food.

She designs and creates **"Eat The Rainbow"** Reward Charts and products to help encourage children to eat a more healthy, colourful and fulfilled diet to help nourish their bodies from the inside out.

Visit Lisa at
www.lisalowndes.biz
to see her range of products

Thank You

Thank you kindly for choosing our book. The journey of collaborating with other Co-Authors across the U.S. and Internationally has been such a great experience both personally and professionally. Together we share a mutual understanding of True stories of abuse, tragedy and heartache leading to strength, hope and happiness.

I'd like to personally thank each co-author for putting their trust in me directing this endeavor and collectively making our voices heard!

Rebecca Adams

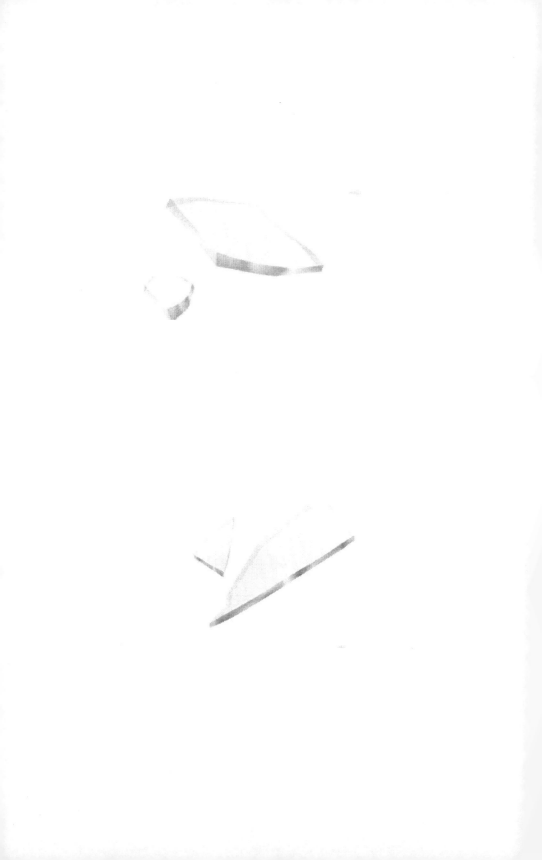

Printed in Poland
by Amazon Fulfillment
Poland Sp. z o.o., Wrocław

64273879R00125